I0410608

Contents

Executive Summary

Calls for criminal justice reform have been mounting in recent years, in large part due to the extraordinarily high levels of incarceration in the United States. Today, the incarcerated population is 4.5 times larger than in 1980, with approximately 2.2 million people in the United States behind bars, including individuals in Federal and State prisons as well as local jails. The push for reform comes from many angles, from the high financial cost of maintaining current levels of incarceration to the humanitarian consequences of detaining more individuals than any other country.

Economic analysis is a useful lens for understanding the costs, benefits, and consequences of incarceration and other criminal justice policies. In this report, we first examine historical growth in criminal justice enforcement and incarceration along with its causes. We then develop a general framework for evaluating criminal justice policy, weighing its crime-reducing benefits against its direct government costs and indirect costs for individuals, families, and communities. Finally, we describe the Administration's holistic approach to criminal justice reform through policies that impact the community, the cell block, and the courtroom.

U.S. incarceration has grown rapidly over the last three and a half decades, driven by changes in criminal justice policy, not underlying changes in crime.

In recent decades, the U.S. incarcerated population has grown dramatically, despite falling crime rates.
- Adjusting for population, the incarceration rate grew by more than 220 percent between 1980 and 2014. The U.S. incarceration rate is higher than the any other country in the OECD, and is more than four times the world average.
- At the same time, crime rates have fallen sharply; between 1980 and 2014 violent crime rates fell by 39 percent and property crime rates fell by 52 percent.
- Economic research has found that incarceration growth is unlikely to be a root cause of the drop in crime. Instead, research finds that the decrease in crime may be attributable to a number of other factors, including demographic changes, changes in policing tactics, and improving economic conditions.

Growth in U.S. incarceration has been fueled by criminal justice policies.
- If prison admission rates and average time served in prison remained the same as they were in 1984, research suggests that State imprisonment rates would have actually declined by 7 percent by 2004, given falling crime rates. Instead, State prison rates increased by over 125 percent.
- Changes in the severity of sentencing and enforcement, which have led to longer sentences and higher conviction rates for nearly all offenses, have been the primary drivers of the incarceration boom.
- Changes in arrest patterns have also likely contributed to incarceration growth. As crime rates have fallen, arrests have also declined but at a slower pace, resulting in increases in arrests

per crime, for both violent and property crimes. Meanwhile, drug arrest rates grew by over 90 percent between 1980 and 2014.

Interactions with the criminal justice system are disproportionately concentrated among Blacks and Hispanics, poor individuals, and individuals with high rates of mental illness and substance abuse.

- Though Blacks and Hispanics represent approximately 30 percent of the population, they comprise over 50 percent of the incarcerated population.
- A large body of research finds that, for similar offenses, Blacks and Hispanics are more likely than Whites to be stopped and searched, arrested, convicted, and sentenced to harsher penalties.
- Approximately 65 percent of prisoners have not completed high school and 14 percent have less than an 8th grade education.
- Over a third of the prison population has received public assistance at some point in their lives, 13 percent grew up in foster care, and over 10 percent experienced homelessness in the year prior to entering prison.
- Over 50 percent of the incarcerated have mental health problems, while approximately 70 percent were regular drug users and 65 percent regularly used alcohol prior to being incarcerated.

Economics can provide a useful lens for thinking about the costs and benefits of criminal justice reform.

Improving safety and reducing crime are central goals of the criminal justice system.

- Though crime rates have declined substantially over recent decades, the benefits of eliminating existing crime are still extensive, likely totaling hundreds of billions of dollars each year.
- The benefits of reducing crime include lowering direct damages to property and medical costs, as well as indirect costs of pain, suffering, fear, reduced quality of life or loss of life.

Criminal justice policies have the capacity to reduce crime, but the aggregate crime-reducing benefits of incarceration are small and decline as the incarcerated population grows.

- Given that the U.S. has the largest prison population in the world, research shows that further increasing the incarcerated population is not likely to materially reduce crime.
- Economic research suggests that longer sentence lengths have little deterrent impact on offenders. A recent paper estimates that a 10 percent increase in average sentence length corresponds to a zero to 0.5 percent decrease in arrest rates.
- Emerging research finds that longer spells of incarceration increase recidivism. A recent study finds that each additional sanction year causes an average increase in future offending of 4 to 7 percentage points.

Investments in police and policies that improve labor market opportunity and educational attainment are likely to have greater crime-reducing benefits than additional incarceration.

- Expanding resources for police has consistently been shown to reduce crime; estimates from economic research suggest that a 10 percent increase in police force size decreases crime by 3 to 10 percent. At the same time, more research is needed to identify and replicate model policing tactics that are marked by trust, transparency, and collaborations between law enforcement and community stakeholders.
- Labor market conditions and increased educational attainment can have large impacts on crime reduction by providing meaningful alternatives to criminal activity. Estimates from research suggest that a 10 percent increase in the high school graduation rate leads to a 9 percent drop in arrest rates, and a 10 percent increase in wages for non-college educated men leads to a 10 to 20 percent reduction in crime rates.

The direct government costs of the criminal justice system are significant.

- Real expenditures on the criminal justice system as a whole total over $270 billion, or $870 per capita and have grown by over 70 percent in the last two decades.
- Real spending on incarceration totaled over $80 billion, or more than $260 per capita. In 2013, 11 states spent more on corrections than on higher education.
- Relative to average rates in the world, the United States employs 2.5 times more corrections officers per capita, while we employ 30 percent fewer police officers per capita.
- The large and increasing costs of the criminal justice system reflect an increase in enforcement over time, and potential adjustments to current policy could provide real savings.

Criminal justice policies also generate a number of indirect costs, or collateral consequences, for individuals with criminal records, their families, and their communities.

- Having a criminal record makes it more difficult to find employment. Recent job application experiments find that applicants with criminal records were 50 percent less likely to receive an interview request or job offer, relative to identical applicants with no criminal record, and these disparities were larger for Black applicants. The formerly incarcerated earn 10 to 40 percent less than similar workers without a history of incarceration.
- The probability that a family is in poverty increases by nearly 40 percent while a father is incarcerated.
- Because incarceration secludes individuals from their families and communities, it decreases the likelihood of marriage and increases the likelihood of divorce.
- It is estimated that more than 5 million children have a parent that has ever been incarcerated, and rates of parental incarceration are 2 to 7 times higher for Black and Hispanic children than White children. Parental incarceration is a strong risk factor for a number of adverse outcomes, including antisocial and violent behavior, mental health problems, school dropout, and unemployment.

Given the total costs, some criminal justice policies, including increased incarceration, fail a cost-benefit test.

- Economic researchers have evaluated the costs and benefits of policies in different criminal justice areas and find that relative to investments in police and education, investments in incarceration are unlikely to be cost-effective.
- Moreover, cost-benefit evaluations of incarceration and sentencing often fail to consider collateral consequences, which would render these policies even more costly.
- CEA conducted "back-of-the-envelope" cost-benefit tests of three policies: increasing incarceration, investing in police, and raising the minimum wage.
    - We find that a $10 billion dollar increase in incarceration spending would reduce crime by 1 to 4 percent (or 55,000 to 340,000 crimes) and have a net societal benefit of -$8 billion to $1 billion dollars.
    - At the same time, a $10 billion dollar investment in police hiring would decrease crime by 5 to 16 percent (440,000 to 1.5 million crimes) have a net societal benefit of $4 to $38 billion dollars.
    - Drawing on literature that finds that higher wages for low-income individuals reduce crime by providing viable and sustainable employment, CEA finds that raising the minimum wage to $12 by 2020 would result in a 3 to 5 percent crime decrease (250,000 to 510,000 crimes) and a societal benefit of $8 to $17 billion dollars.

The Administration is committed to a holistic approach to criminal justice reform that creates a fairer and smarter system in the community, the cell block and the courtroom.

- Investments in early childhood, including limiting out of school suspensions, can reduce involvement with the criminal justice system, while increasing resources for police, community policing, and enhanced police transparency can improve community safety and build trust.
- In order to foster law enforcement agencies that both build trust and keep communities safe, investments in police hiring should also be accompanied by support for community policing strategies and evaluation of best practices.
- Addressing criminal record employment restrictions, through expanding record expungement, "banning-the-box", and limiting blanket criminal record exclusions in occupational licensing laws, as well as improving access to health care and housing can help reduce the collateral consequences of convictions.
- Working with Congress and the States to rationalize the ways we impose sentences, and reduce high rates of incarceration, will make our criminal justice system fairer, smarter, and more cost-effective. To further these goals, the Administration is also working with State and local jurisdictions to implement new approaches to fines, fees, and bail that do not criminalize poverty.
- Fixing the conditions in the cell block and offering more job training for inmates can reduce barriers to reentry and decrease recidivism.

Introduction

In recent decades, the criminal justice system in the United States has expanded dramatically. Since 1980, the number of people incarcerated in the U.S. has grown by nearly 350 percent, resulting in approximately 2.2 million people behind bars.[1] Today, the United States incarcerates more people than any other country in the world, and our per-capita incarceration rate is more than four times the world average.

As the incarcerated population has climbed, the crime rate in the United States has declined dramatically. Violent crime has fallen by 39 percent and property crimes have been cut in half over the past three and a half decades.[2] Yet research has established that rising incarceration is not principally responsible for the reduction in crime, and that higher levels of imprisonment have occurred despite—not because of—changes in underlying criminal activity. Though there is no collective consensus about the causes of the decline in crime, several factors may have contributed to the crime drop including demographic changes, changes in policing tactics, and improving economic conditions. A large body of economic research shows that incarceration has only a small impact on crime reduction, and that this impact diminishes as the incarcerated population grows.

Instead, the surge in incarceration has been driven by changes in criminal justice policies. Policies enacted at the Federal and State levels emphasizing harsher sentencing rules (such as the more frequent use of mandatory minimums and "three strikes" rules) and greater enforcement of criminal sanctions have led to longer prison sentences and higher conviction rates. The upsurge in incarceration, together with a growing recognition of the costs of current criminal justice policies, have led many policymakers, researchers, and advocates, across the political spectrum, to conclude that the criminal justice system needs to be comprehensively reformed.

Within this context, economics can provide a valuable lens for evaluating the costs and benefits of criminal justice policy. The criminal justice system has clear benefits: the total social cost of crime in America likely totals hundreds of billions of dollars each year, and the criminal justice system plays an important role in reducing crime and maintaining the safety of citizens.

However, the criminal justice system also carries substantial costs. In 2012, real expenditures on the criminal justice system totaled over $274 billion, or $870 per capita, a 74 percent increase relative to spending in 1993.[3] In 2013, 11 states spent more on corrections than on higher education (Mitchell and Leachman 2014).

---

[1] Bureau of Justice Statistics. 1980-2014. "Prisoners" Series. U.S. Department of Justice; Bureau of Justice Statistics. 1980-2014. "Jail Inmates at Midyear" Series. U.S. Department of Justice;

[2] Federal Bureau of Investigation. 1980-2014. "Crime in the United States – Uniform Crime Reports." U.S. Department of Justice.

[3] Real expenditures are in 2015 dollars.

In addition to its direct costs, the criminal justice system also imposes substantial collateral consequences on individuals with criminal records, their families, and their communities. Having a criminal record makes it more difficult to find employment and depresses earnings. Criminal sanctions can also have negative consequences for individuals' health, debt, transportation, housing, and food security. These consequences can add up to large and lasting negative impacts for incarcerated individuals' families and communities. The probability that a family is living in poverty increases by nearly 40 percent while a father in is prison, and children with incarcerated parents face an increased risk of a variety of adverse outcomes, including antisocial and violent behavior and lower educational attainment (Johnson 2009).

These costs fall most heavily on Black and Hispanic men, poor individuals, and individuals with high rates of mental illness and substance abuse. Although Black and Hispanic Americans account for only 30 percent of the population, they comprise over 50 percent of the incarcerated population (U.S. Census; Carson 2015). One-third of the prison population has received public assistance, and one in ten incarcerated Americans were homeless in the year before entering prison (James and Glaze 2006). Criminal justice sanctions can compound existing disadvantages for these populations, reinforcing patterns of intergenerational poverty.

Recognizing the size of these costs, the Administration is committed to meaningful reform of the criminal justice system, and has taken actions to improve underlying conditions in the community, the courtroom, and the cell block. The Administration has invested in communities to address the root causes and consequences of involvement in the justice system. The Administration has expanded access to early childhood education and targeted prevention programs for youth, which have been found to significantly reduce criminal behavior later in life. In addition, the Administration has worked to improve community-police relations by providing extra resources for law enforcement, investing in community policing, and increasing police transparency.

In the courtroom, the Administration has worked to enhance common sense sentencing reforms by reducing disparities in mandatory minimums for crack and powder cocaine possession, and modernizing Federal sentencing guidelines for drug crimes. New grants have been issued to assist States in reducing the burden that fees, fines, and bail impose on low-income Americans. And the Administration has invested in court diversion programs that support Veterans and individuals living with mental health conditions and addiction.[4]

Finally, the Administration has invested in rehabilitation programs in prisons and jails. Reentry programs have been advanced by expanding education and job-training programs for those who have served their time. The Administration has also prioritized reforming solitary confinement practices, which can lead to negative long-term consequences for those who are exposed to them and for the communities to which these individuals return.

---

[4] Court diversion programs allow defendants to avoid court sanctions or court proceedings if the defendant meets prescribed conditions, which may include drug treatment or rehabilitation.

This report builds on this progress by offering economic perspectives on criminal justice reform. The report first analyzes the growth in the incarcerated population, and finds that changes to criminal justice policies—not underlying changes in crime—are principally responsible for this trend. The report also examines the relative costs and benefits of different criminal justice policies, and concludes that investments in police, education, and jobs programs are more cost-effective than increasing incarceration. Finally, the report outlines several promising areas for reform, and highlights recent actions taken by the Administration to holistically improve the criminal justice system.

I. Defining the Landscape: Current Criminal Justice Policies and Historical Context

Over the last three and a half decades, the criminal justice system in the United States has rapidly expanded. Most striking is the growth in incarceration; the number of people behind bars grew by 350 percent between 1980 and 2014 (Figure 1).

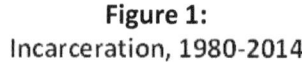

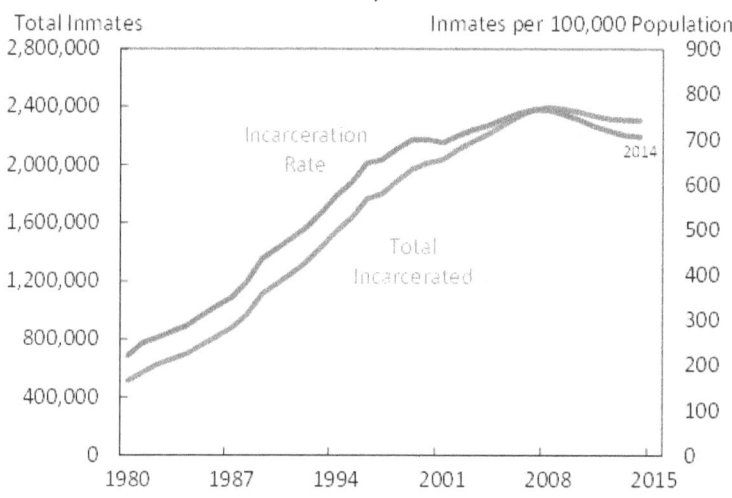

Figure 1:
Incarceration, 1980-2014

Source: Bureau of Justice Statistics, CEA calculations.

Mirroring the rise in incarceration, direct expenditures on the criminal justice system have increased substantially. Real total government spending on the criminal justice system grew by 74 percent between 1993 and 2012, to $274 billion. Similarly, in 2012, real per capita criminal justice spending was $872 per year, up 43 percent over the same time period. Real expenditures on corrections were $83 billion, representing over a quarter of total criminal justice spending in 2012 (Figure 2).[5]

---

[5]All real dollar figures in this report use 2015 dollar values. A more detailed discussion of direct government expenditures on the criminal justice system can be found in the section on "Direct Government Spending on the Criminal Justice System."

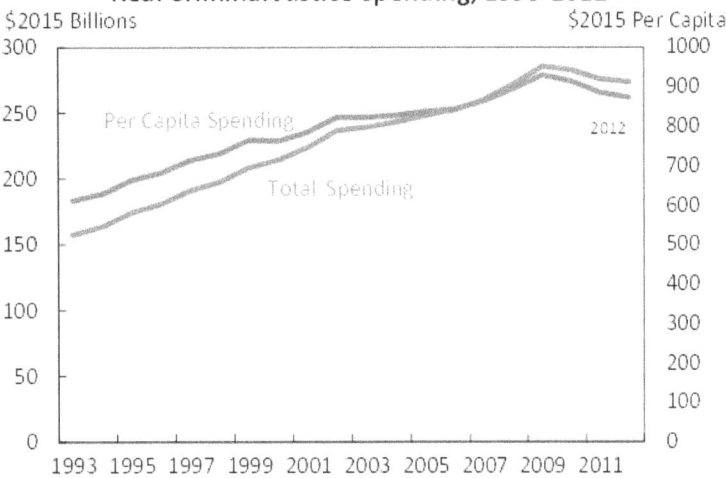

Figure 2:
Real Criminal Justice Spending, 1993-2012

Over the same time period, violent crime rates declined dramatically, falling by 39 percent since 1980 and by 52 percent from their peak in 1991 (Figure 3). Despite the correlation between declining crime and increasing incarceration, rising incarceration is not a fundamental driver of the decline in crime. A large body of economic research shows that incarceration has only a small aggregate impact on crime reduction, and that this impact falls as the incarcerated population grows.[6] In fact, because rising incarceration did not drive the reduction in crime, the rise of prison population is all the more striking since crime was actually falling.

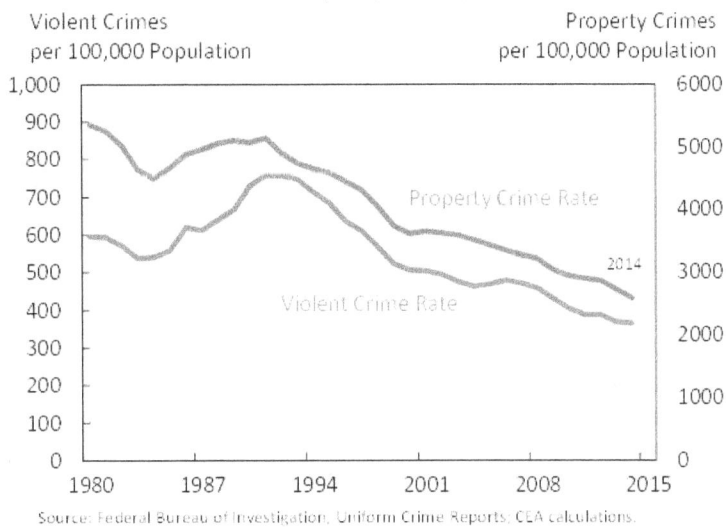

Figure 3:
Violent and Property Crime, 1980-2014

---

[6] The impact of incarceration on crime reduction is discussed in detail in Section II.B of the report.

A number of other factors have contributed to the decline in crime, though researchers have not reached consensus on the relative importance of these causes. Improvements in economic conditions through rising incomes and falling unemployment have likely played a role. Demographic changes also likely play a part; the youth proportion of the U.S. population (ages 15-30) declined by 12 percent between 1980 and 2013, reducing the general propensity for criminal behavior which is more prevalent among young people. Improvements in police tactics and technology used in policing may have also played a role. Other potential explanations include declines in alcohol consumption, decreases in "crack" cocaine use, and a reduction in exposure to lead (see Roeder, Eisen, and Bowling 2015 and citations below).[7]

In this section, we explore the underlying mechanics of the rise in incarceration in the United States. We find that the primary drivers of incarceration growth have been an increase in conviction rates given arrest and a rise in average sentence length. Finally, we examine the characteristics of the population impacted by mass incarceration, a group that is disproportionately represented by poor minority men, as well as individuals with a history of mental illness and other health and social risk factors.

Incarceration Growth and the Criminal Justice System

There are several steps in the criminal justice process, including interactions with police, arrest, declaration of criminal charges, court proceedings, conviction, and sentencing. Criminal justice system actions at each step of this process have the potential to change the size and composition of the incarcerated population. Criminal justice policies, not changes in underlying crime, account for nearly all of the growth in the incarcerated population in recent decades (e.g. Raphael and Stoll 2013b; Neal and Rick 2014).

Policing and Arrests

The initial entry point into the criminal justice system is arrest. More policing can potentially lead to more arrests and contribute to rising prison admissions. Growth in the total police force, however, has slowed in recent years after increasing by over 20 percent between 1980 and 1995. After factoring in population growth, total growth in policing rates, the proportion of police to residents, has been flat over the last three and a half decades.[8] Given these patterns, it is unlikely that changes in police staffing levels are a primary driver of the incarceration boom (Figure 4).

---

[7] Though there is no consensus about the relative importance of these factors, there is a large body of research on these topics. Further citations for the following topics include: income and unemployment (e.g. Raphael and Winter-Ebmer 2001; Gould, Weinberg, and Mustard 2002); demographic changes and aging of the population (e.g. Levitt 1999; Tittle et al., 2003; Blumstein and Nakamura 2009); police technology and tactics (e.g. Weisburd et al. 2010; Braga, Papachristos and Hureau 2014; Roeder, Eisen, and Bowling 2015); declines in alcohol consumption (e.g. Markowitz 2000); decreases in "crack" cocaine use (e.g. Fryer et al. 2013; Evans, Garthwaite, and Moore 2012); and reduction in lead exposure (e.g. Reyes 2007).

[8] Figure 4 uses data from two different sources; Bureau of Justice Statistics (BJS) Employment and Expenditure Extracts (1980-1994) and the Federal Bureau of Investigation (FBI) Uniform Crime Reports (1995-2014). We utilize full-time equivalent police counts from BJS and divide these by the Census population to create rates. For the FBI

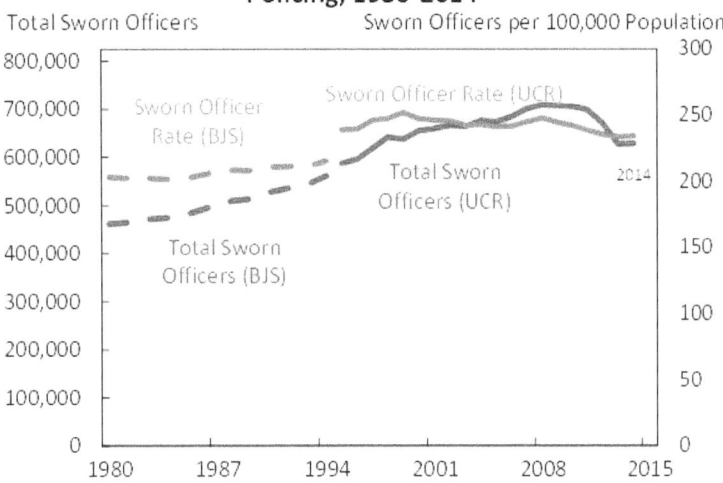

Figure 4:
Policing, 1980-2014

Source: Federal Bureau of Investigation, Uniform Crime Reports, Bureau of Justice Statistics, Employment and Expenditures Extracts, Census Bureau, CEA calculations.

At the same time, descriptive data suggest that the likelihood of arrest has increased modestly for violent and property crimes despite falling crime rates. Between 1980 and 2014 both violent crime rates and violent crime arrests fell, but because crime decreased by more than arrests, the likelihood of being arrested for a given crime increased. A similar phenomenon occurred with property crimes. In aggregate, the rate of arrests per violent crime and arrests for property crime have both increased by approximately 20 percent since 1980 (Figure 5).[9]

---

series, we scale officer counts by population of districts reporting. These data sets come from different surveys of police departments and use different methodologies to create aggregate estimates of police and police per capita. Because of this, there is a break in the data series between 1994 and 1995, and each section of the data series should be considered separately. Per capita policing is flat in each data portion.

[9] Arrests can only be benchmarked to crimes for categories of crimes that are reported, or violent and property crimes. Crime rates for other offenses are not reported or tracked comprehensively.

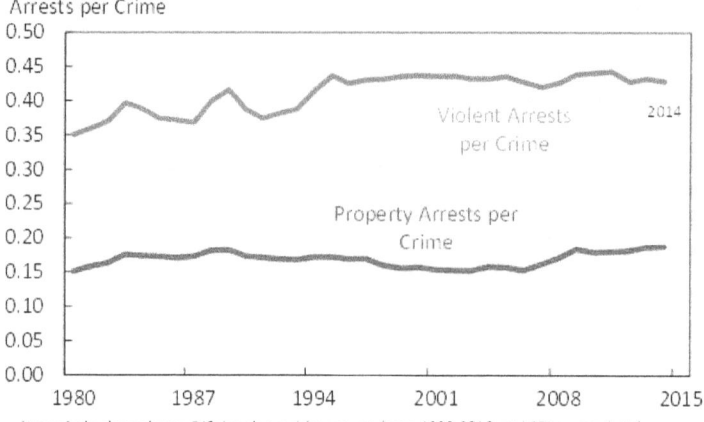

Figure 5:
Arrests per Crime, 1980-2014

Note: As in chart above, BJS data is used for arrests from 1980-2012 and FBI arrest data is used between 2013-2014.
Source: Bureau of Justice Statistics Arrest Data Tool; Federal Bureau of Investigation, Uniform Crime Reports; CEA calculations.

An important exception to the declining trend in arrests is arrests for drug crimes, which have grown at a rapid pace. Between 1980 and 2014, drug arrest rates increased by over 90 percent, and this dramatic rise has contributed to rising incarceration rates. In 2006, the rate of drug arrests reached a peak and approximately 2 million people were arrested for drug crimes that year (Figure 6).[10] Though the trend has partially reversed in recent years, the dramatic rise in drug arrests has contributed to rising prison admission rates for drug crimes.

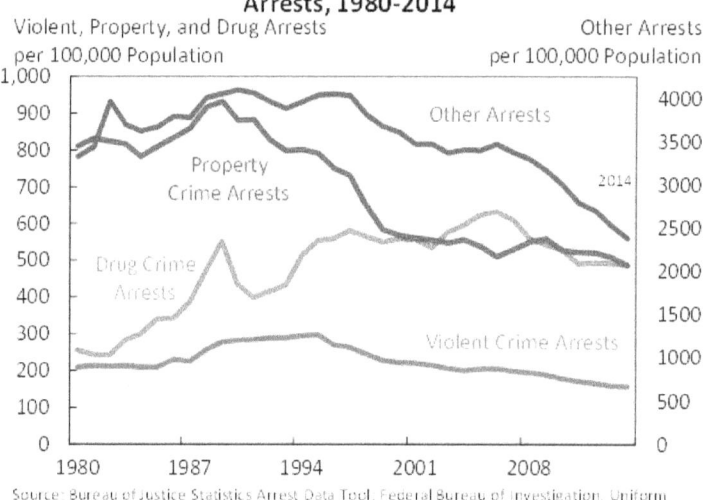

Figure 6:
Arrests, 1980-2014

Source: Bureau of Justice Statistics Arrest Data Tool; Federal Bureau of Investigation, Uniform Crime Reports; CEA calculations.

---

[10] Figure 6 applies Index I crime definitions to the arrest reports for violent and property crimes. Drug crimes include drug possession and trafficking. Other crimes include fraud, sexual assault, simple assault, weapons offenses, arson DUIs and other miscellaneous offenses. BJS data applies assumptions to extend arrest rates from the subset of reporting agencies to national rates and because of this we use BJS data from 1980-2012. FBI UCR data is used for 2013-2014. Because police reporting increases substantially over time, the two data sets are comparable in recent years.

After being arrested and charged with a crime, a defendant may be detained in jail while awaiting court proceedings. The defendant then faces conviction or acquittal, or charges may be dismissed. Thus, case disposition represents another decision point that may influence trends in incarceration. Convictions have dramatically increased over the last several decades, and rising rates of conviction are a root cause of the increase in incarceration in the United States. Between 1986 and 2006, total conviction rates in State courts (per 100,000 residents) increased by 56 percent. The largest increase occurred among drug trafficking convictions – which more than doubled – while violent crime convictions increased somewhat and property crime convictions were little changed.[11] The rise in convictions for drug crimes is particularly striking; by 2006 there were over 250,000 drug convictions in State courts, outpacing convictions for violent and property crimes. Since their 2006 peak, drug arrests have leveled, declining by 23 percent. Conviction rates for other crimes, which include simple assaults, fraud, sexual assault, weapons offenses, and drunk driving, also increased by 94 percent (Figure 7).[12]

Figure 7:
Felony Convictions in State Courts, 1986-2006

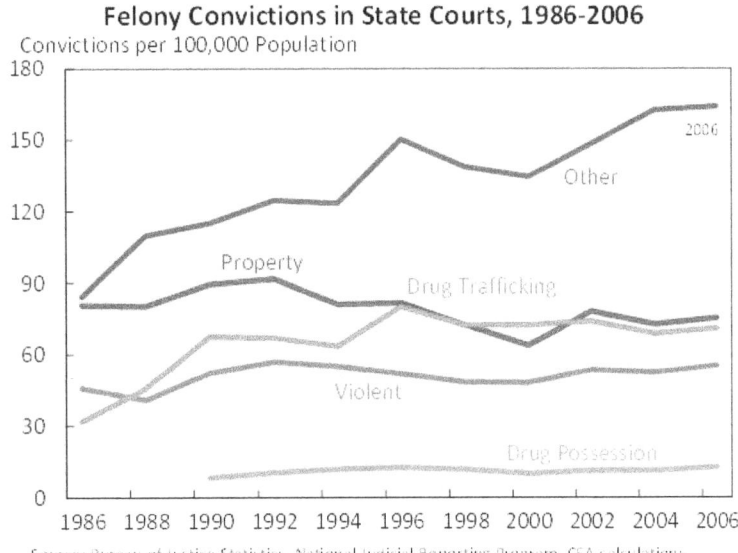

Source: Bureau of Justice Statistics, National Judicial Reporting Program, CEA calculations.

Although convictions are partly a function of the severity of a given crime and the strength of the case against the defendant, it is unlikely that the secular rise in total convictions over the last several decades can be explained by case-specific factors (Raphael and Stoll 2013b). Instead, changes in practice and policy of local government, prosecutors, and the court system have likely driven the increase in convictions.

---

[11] For consistency with crime statistics, the violent and property categories used here are analogous to the FBI Index I categories and do not align with the National Judicial Reporting Program categories. Violent crime includes murder, rape and robbery, while property crime includes burglary, larceny and motor vehicle theft.

[12] Conviction categories map to arrest categories in Figure 7. Drug crimes are split into possession and trafficking because possession has only been tracked since 1990 and total drug crimes cannot be derived for earlier years.

In particular, the increase in convictions likely reflects the "get tough on crime" movement in the 1980s and 1990s that caused cultural changes in the criminal justice system. During this time period, a series of Federal and State laws increased sentence lengths, through new mandatory minimum penalties, repeat offender laws, and restrictions on parole releases (Travis, Redburn, and Western 2014, Ch. 3). Additionally, through the 1984 crime bill, the federal government banned parole. Moreover, the "War on Drugs" expanded resources for fighting drug crime and placed an emphasis on incarcerating individuals arrested for drug crimes (Albonetti 2016). Popular support for harsher sanctions for offenders also influenced elections for judges, often translating to higher conviction rates (Weiss 2006).

The growth in incarceration admissions has been driven by rising total convictions, not by an increase in the relative proportion of convictions that result in a prison sentence (Figure 8). Over time, the fraction of State court convictions that resulted in an incarceration sentence was roughly constant. Similarly, the proportions of State court convictions that resulted in jail or probation sentences were also unchanged.

Figure 8:
Percent of State Court Convictions by Sentence Type, 1986-2006

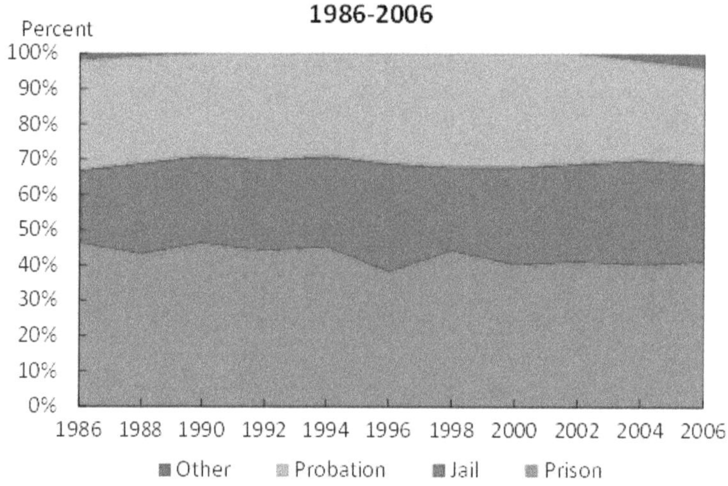

Source: Bureau of Justice Statistics, National Judicial Reporting Program, CEA calculations.

While many common conceptions of the criminal justice system focus on trials to decide guilt or innocence, the vast majority of convicted defendants agree to plea bargains rather than a jury trial. Because guilty pleas can involve concessions from prosecutors, it is possible that they may lead to probation or shorter sentences (Devers 2011). However, in practice, the plea bargaining process may provide defendants with limited negotiating power. While it is possible that defendants rationally weigh the risks and benefits of going to trial before accepting plea deals, in an environment with widespread plea bargaining and broad prosecutorial discretion, defendants may be pressured to enter a plea. In extreme cases, defendants who are afraid of risky trial outcomes may even plead guilty to charges for crimes that they did not commit (Rakoff 2014).

However, changes in the manner of conviction over time, whether a plea bargain or a trial, are also unlikely to have caused the increase in convictions leading to incarceration. Over 90 percent of convictions in State courts are guilty pleas, with only 5 to 10 percent of convictions determined at trial. These proportions have been relatively constant over recent decades, and therefore, high rates of guilty plea convictions are unlikely to be driving the boom in incarceration admissions (Figure 9).

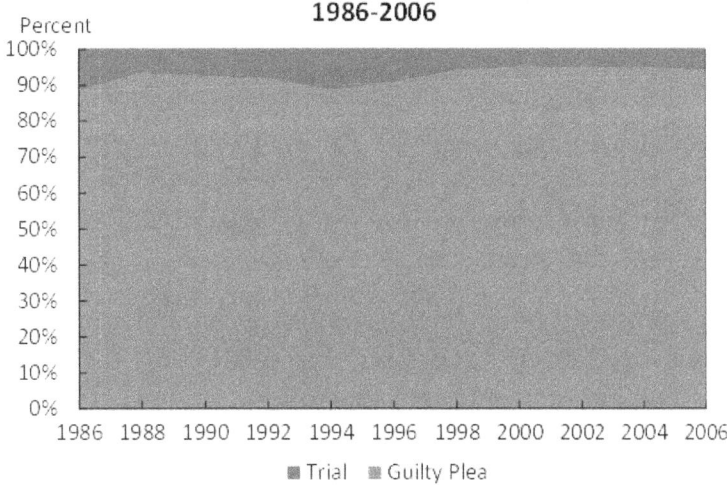

Figure 9:
Percent of State Court Convictions by Method,
1986-2006

Source: Bureau of Justice Statistics, National Judicial Reporting Program, CEA calculations.

Changes in total conviction rates, the proportion of defendants convicted for the crimes charged, have increased the likelihood of prison admission and inflated the prison population. Below, Figures 9 and 10 show estimates of changes in the number of people admitted to prison per arrest and time served in prison between 1984 and 2004 for different crime types, adapted from Raphael and Stoll (2013b). These calculations show that the number of people admitted to prison per arrest have more than doubled for most crimes and have tripled for drug crimes (Figure 10).[13]

---

[13] Per crime calculations in Figure 9 are taken from Raphael and Stoll (2013b) that joins FBI Uniform Crime Report data on arrests and prison admissions from the National Corrections Reporting Program data. Because NCRP data covers a subset of states, these estimates reflect the best available data but may not generalize to national trends. "Average" is calculated only from the distribution of conviction rates for the subset of crimes shown.

Figure 10:
Percent Change in Prison Admissions per Arrest, 1984-2004

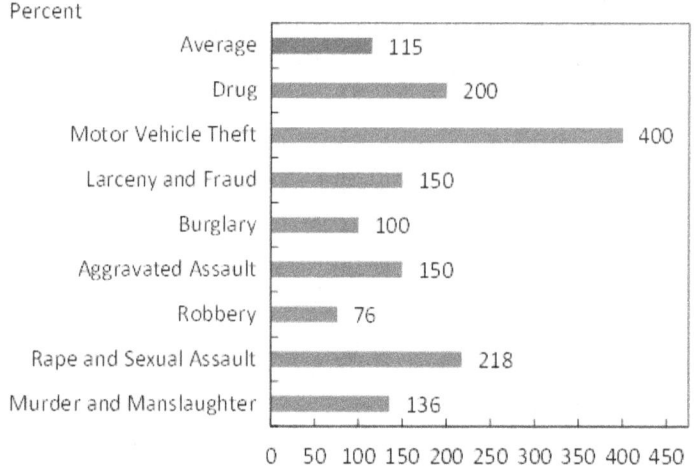

Source: Reproduced from Table 2.2 and 2.3 and Figure 2.4 in Raphael and Stoll (2013b), CEA Calculations.

Longer sentences have also contributed to today's high incarceration rates. Between 1984 and 2004 most crimes shown experienced a substantial increase in time served (Figure 11).[14] Despite a sharp increase in the number of people convicted of drug crimes, time served for drug crimes across State and Federal prisons remained roughly constant, declining by 6 percent, with an average incarceration time of 21 months in 2004 (Figure 11). The net impact of these changes, a substantial increase in sentence length for most offenses and sharp rise in convictions for all crimes, was a large contributor to incarceration growth (Travis, Western, and Redburn 2014, Ch. 2).

---

[14] Time served measures the actual amount of time an individual is incarcerated and is less than or equal to an assigned sentence, given the possibility of early release on parole. Per crime calculations in Figure 10 are taken from Raphael and Stoll (2013b) that analyzes releases in the National Corrections Reporting Program data for State incarceration. As in the prior chart, this chart uses NCRP data that covers a subset of states. The "Average" calculation uses the distribution of crime categories also provided by the authors for the subset of crimes in the figure.

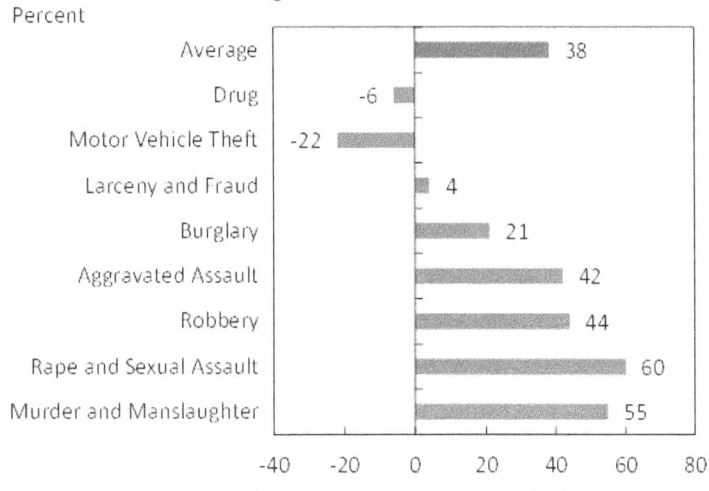

Figure 11:
Percent Change in Time Served, 1984-2004

Source: Reproduced from Table 2.4 and Figure 2.4 in Raphael and Stoll (2013b); CEA Calculations.

Relative to the analysis of all prisoners, changes in Federal prisons show different patterns in time served (Figure 12 below). According to analysis by The Pew Charitable Trusts, time served in Federal prisons increased for all offenses between 1988 and 2012. In contrast to the small change in time served for drug crimes in all prisons, time served for drug offenses in Federal prisons more than doubled over the last two decades (The Pew Charitable Trusts 2015).

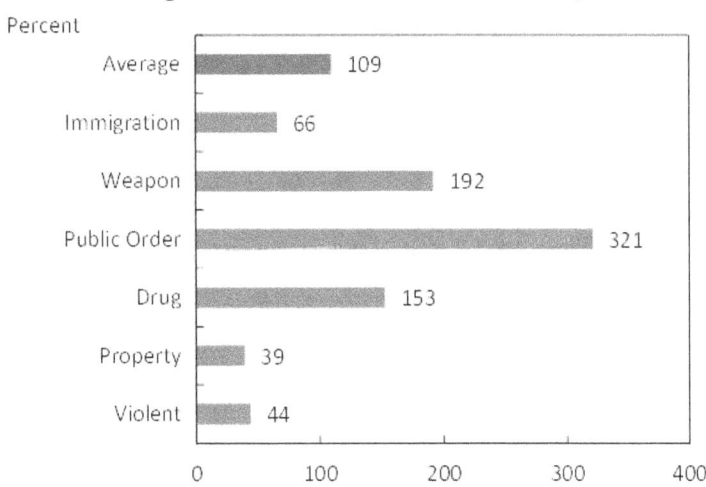

Figure 12:
Percent Change in Time Served in Federal Prison, 1988-2012

Source: Reproduced from Figure 1 in The Pew Charitable Trusts (2015); CEA Calculations.

Relative to other factors, rising prison admission rates have been the most important contributor to the increase in incarceration. Raphael and Stoll (2013b) decompose the growth in the prison population into changes in crime rates, prison admissions and time served. If criminal justice policies remained the same as they were in 1984, State imprisonment rates would have actually declined by 7 percent by 2004, given falling crime rates. Instead, State prison rates increased by over 125 percent. After accounting for falling crime rates, over two-thirds of this increase was attributable to rising prison admission rates, and 14 percent to increases in time served. In Federal prisons, longer sentences and rising admissions rates have been equally important, each accounting for approximately 20 percent of the growth in the Federal prison rate that is not due to changes in crime (Figure 13).[15]

Figure 13:
Decomposition of Change in Incarceration, 1984-2009

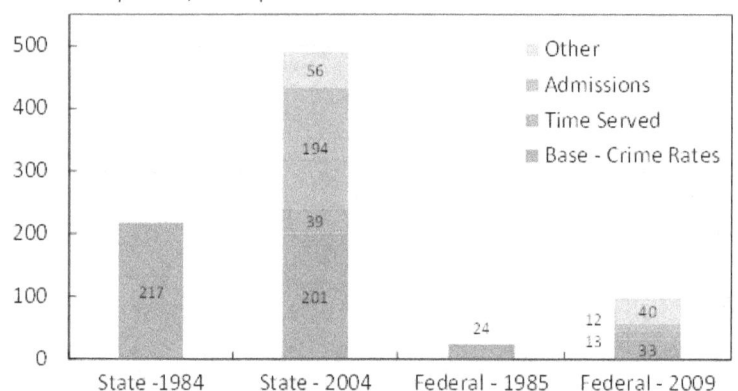

Note: This decomposition represents the results from a simulation of steady states of incarceration in each reference year using variation in policies. 'Other' here is variation in simulated incarceration that is not captured by observed crime rates, or policies related to prison admissions and time served.
Source: Reproduced from Figure 3.1 and 3.3 in Raphael and Stoll (2013b), CEA Calculations.

Local, State, and Federal Incarceration Trends

The combination of dramatic increases in admissions rates and the multiplicative effect of longer sentences has led to a sharp rise in the incarcerated population. The share of the population that is incarcerated has more than tripled since 1980 and today stands at approximately 2.2 million people behind bars. State prisoners represent the majority of the incarcerated population, at 58 percent, while a third are detained in local jails and approximately 9 percent are in Federal prisons. Despite its small size, the Federal prison population grew the fastest over this period, increasing by over 755 percent (Figure 14).

---

[15] The incarceration rates and changes shown above are simulated from analysis in Raphael and Stoll (2013b). Each component of the 2004 bar shows the contribution of 2004 policy to the 2004 rate. For example, if only crime rates had changed, 2004 prison rates would decrease by 16, while changes in admissions rates increased the incarceration rate by 194.

Figure 14:
Incarceration, 1980-2014

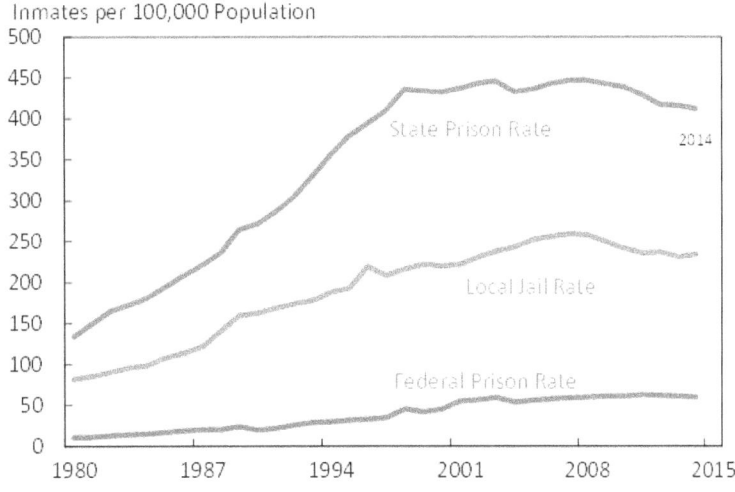

Source: Bureau of Justice Statistics, CEA calculations.

As convictions have increased, the number of individuals detained in local jails while awaiting a conviction or acquittal in their case has also risen. Between 1983 and 2014 the proportion of jail inmates who had been convicted grew by 90 percent, but was dwarfed by the rise in jail inmates not convicted of a crime, which grew by 200 percent (Figure 15). Growth in the unconvicted jail population has been heightened by an increase in the use of financial bail that many cannot afford;[16] in 1990, 53 percent of felony defendants in large counties were assigned bail, and by 2009, this proportion had grown to 72 percent.[17] Many defendants have limited resources and are not able to post bail, remaining incarcerated while awaiting conviction or acquittal (CEA 2015b).

---

[16] Financial bail schedules increase with the severity of crimes and are meant to increase the likelihood of detainment for more dangerous offenders. However, uniform bail schedules are a crude way to screen pretrial defendants for their risk of flight or to the community because it does not consider an individual's ability to pay any given bail assignment. In effect, standardized bail schedules often detain the poorest rather than the most dangerous offenders. Instead, risk-assessment tools and modeling can be used to determine non-financial release based on the relative risks posed by a particular individual (see CEA 2015b).

[17] Bureau of Justice Statistics. 1990-2009. "Felony Defendants in Large Counties." *Department of Justice.*

Figure 15:
Convicted and Unconvicted Inmates in Local Jails, 1983-2014

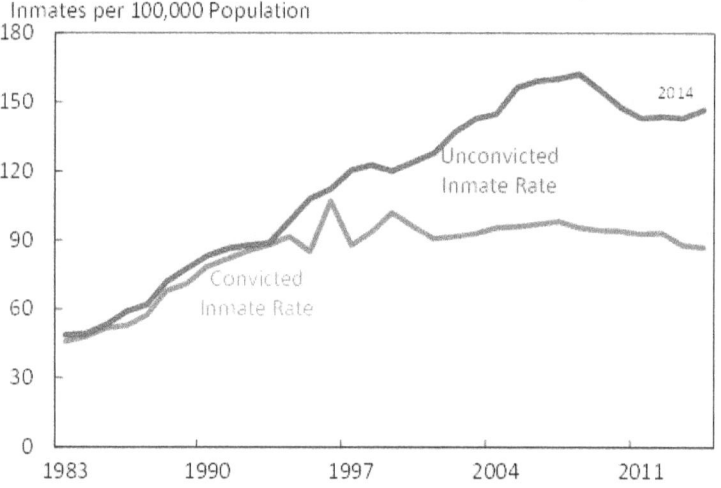

Note: Data for 1989 and 1994 were not available and were imputed from adjacent values.
Source: Bureau of Justice Statistics, CEA calculations.

In terms of offense characteristics, the State and Federal prison population have pronounced differences. Approximately half of State prisoners are serving sentences for violent crimes, while in Federal prisons, half of prisoners are serving sentences for nonviolent drug crimes (Figure 16).[18] The Federal and State prison populations have stark contrasts in other crime categories as well; while 19 percent of State prisoners are incarcerated for property crimes, this proportion is only 6 percent for Federal prisoners. In the Federal prison population, the proportion of other offenses, which include weapons and public order violations, has more than doubled since 1990.

Figure 16:
Prison Population by Crime, 1990-2014

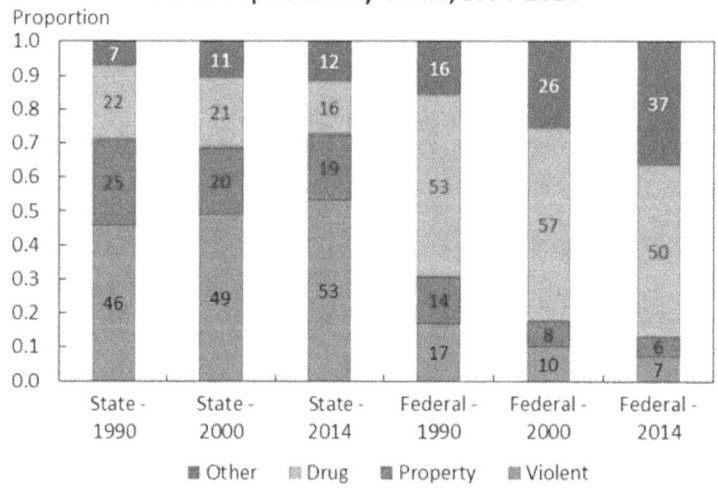

Source: Bureau of Justice Statistics, CEA calculations.

---

[18] As in charts above, crime categories are derived Bureau of Justice Statistics definitions for violent, property and drug crimes. Other crime includes all other categories of offenses, such as weapons offenses, sexual assault, simple assault, and fraud.

There are also large geographic differences in incarceration rates across States. Below, a map shows the distribution of total sentenced State and Federal prisoners per 100,000 residents. In 2014, the national sentenced imprisonment rate was 471 prisoners per 100,000 residents.[19] Southern states tend to have higher prison rates, with the highest rate of imprisonment at 816 in Louisiana, more than 1.7 times the national rate. At the other end of the distribution, Maine had the lowest prison rate of 153, less than a third of the national rate (Figure 17).

Figure 17:

Imprisonment Rates for Sentenced Prisoners Under
Jurisdiction of State Correctional Authorities

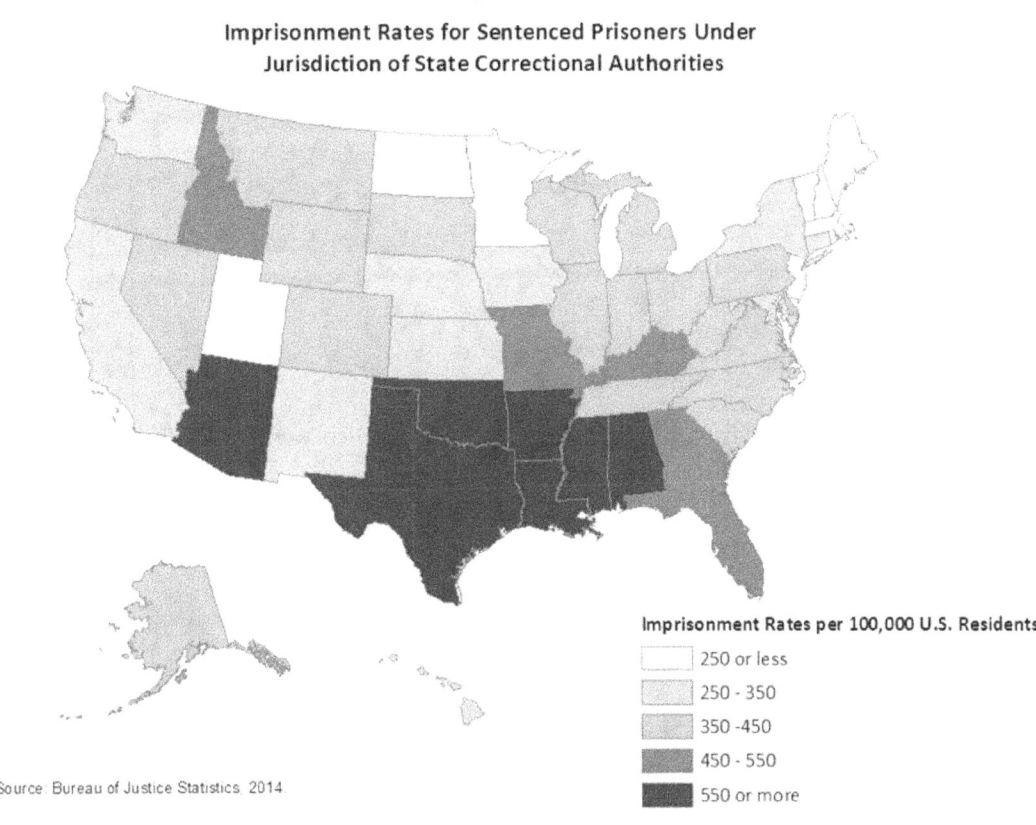

Source: Bureau of Justice Statistics, 2014

Imprisonment Rates per 100,000 U.S. Residents
- 250 or less
- 250 - 350
- 350 -450
- 450 - 550
- 550 or more

U.S. incarceration is even more striking when compared to incarceration in other countries. In fact, the United States incarcerates over 20 percent of the world's prisoners despite having less than 5 percent of the world's population (Census 2015; Walmsley 2016). Adjusting for population, Figure 18 displays a descending ranking of incarceration rates for 20 countries with population over 200,000.[20] The United States outranks all other countries on this list, with an incarceration rate of 698, and the U.S. incarceration rate is over four times the world average rate (Walmsley 2016).

---

[19] Sentenced prisoner counts include prisoners with sentences longer than 1 year under the jurisdiction of State or Federal correctional facilities.

[20] Several small island countries have high incarceration rates, in part because their populations are so small. In 2015, Seychelles (population 89,000) had the highest incarceration rate in the world at 799 incarcerated individuals per 100,000 residents (World Bank 2016; Walmsley 2016). This chart excludes territories and countries with fewer than 200,000 residents.

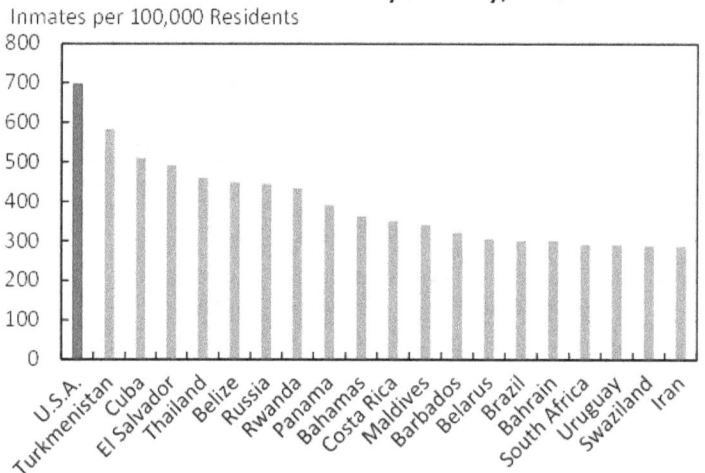

Figure 18:
Incarceration Rate by Country, 2015

Note: Includes 20 countries with highest incarceration rate. Ranking excludes territories and countries with populations less than 200,000.
Source: World Prison Population List.

Recidivism

There is significant churn in the incarcerated population, with over 600,000 prisoners released each year. As the prison population has grown, so has the number of prison releases, increasing by 300 percent since 1980 (Figure 19). Though time served in prison has increased, most prisoners can expect to spend less than five years in prison for a single crime (Raphael and Stoll 2013b), and short-to-medium length spells of incarceration lead to the release of more than a quarter of the incarcerated population annually.

This process is amplified by local jails that typically have higher turnover and hold inmates for shorter periods of time; time served in jails averages 23 days and has increased by over 60 percent over the last three decades (Subramanian et al. 2015). While there are approximately 740,000 inmates in local jails, the total number of jail admissions was 11.4 million in 2014, translating to over 25,000 individuals released on a daily basis (Minton and Zheng 2015).[21]

---

[21] CEA calculated daily release levels by calculating daily admissions from total admissions and subtracting the average daily population in local jails.

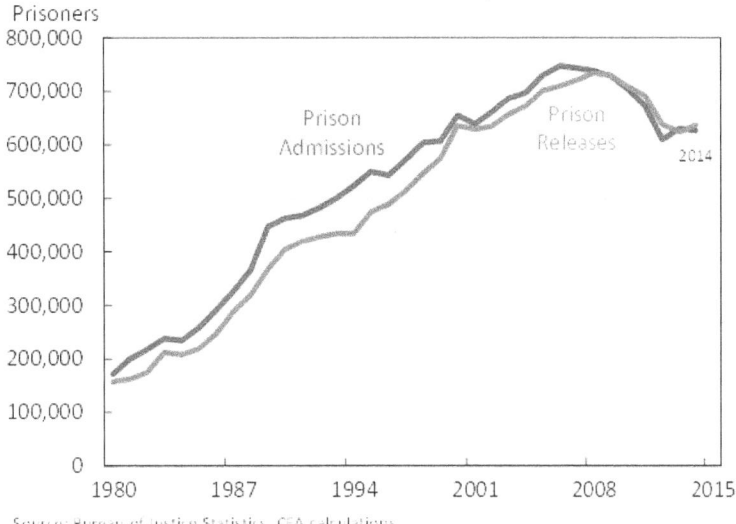

Figure 19:
Prison Admissions and Releases, 1980-2014

Prison releases can contribute to subsequent prison admissions by expanding the population under parole supervision, if there is a high risk that individuals are readmitted to prison for technical violations of parole or other low-level offenses.[22] The State parole population increased by 170 percent between 1984 and 2004 to over 680,000 individuals—about 30 percent of the size of the incarcerated population in that year. In 2004, new court commitments accounted for 60 percent of prison admissions, while parole violations comprised 30 percent and probation violations represented 10 percent. New prison admissions due to technical parole violations have also risen; between 1984 and 2004, the prison admission rate for technical parole violations increased by over 200 percent (Raphael and Stoll 2013b).

Total 5 year recidivism rates for State prisoners are over 70 percent, including both new court convictions and arrests (Durose, Cooper, and Snyder 2014). These high rates of reoffending have amplified growth in the incarcerated population and created a revolving door in prisons.

Below, Figure 20 shows rates of re-offending derived from survey data of individuals who are incarcerated, through measuring the criminal history of those in custody. The first column shows that about a quarter of admitted prisoners do not have a prior incarceration sentence before entering prison or jail. Of the three-quarters entering custody who have a prior sentence, about a third did not have any violent convictions for either their current sentence or prior sentences. The median admitted inmate has two prior incarceration sentences, and 15 percent have served more than five prior sentences.

---

[22] A technical violation of parole occurs when a parolee does not comply with supervision conditions, including employed, attending parole officer meetings, completing substance abuse or other treatment sessions, and/or fulfilling community service requirements. Behaviors that qualify as technical violations of parole differ by state, but typically do not include arrests or charges for new criminal or misdemeanor offenses (Lawrence 2008).

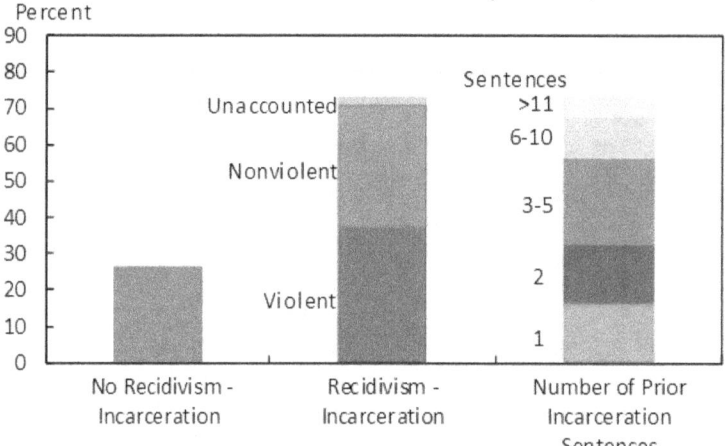

Figure 20:
Recidivism Rates for the Incarcerated Population, 2002-2004

Note: This chart measure recidivism through tracking prior criminal sentences of incarcerated individuals in the survey of State and Federal prisoners (2004) and inmates in Local Jails (2002).
Source: James and Glaze (2006), Bureau of Justice Statistics, CEA Calculations.

In Figure 21, recidivism is measured not through the incarceration history of individuals entering prisons or jails, but by following the cohort of individuals released from State prisons in 2005. This measure includes both arrests and convictions that lead to future incarceration, and shows that roughly half of reoffending over a five year horizon occurs within the first year of release. Within five years, 77 percent of released prisoners have been re-arrested and 55 percent have been convicted of an offense that resulted in a return to prison.

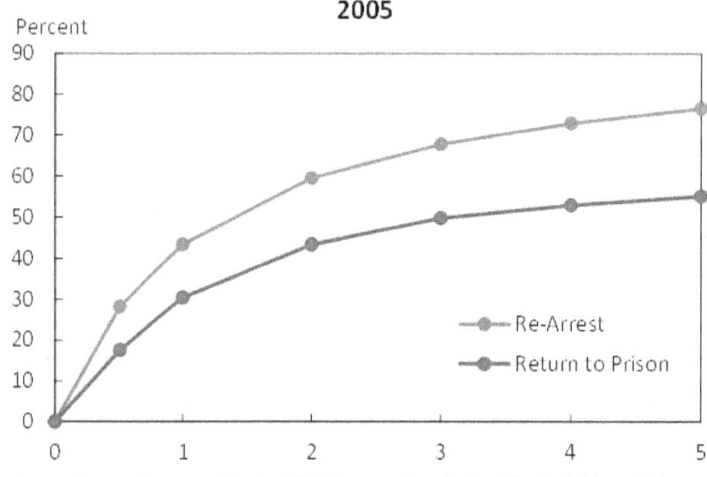

Figure 21:
Cumulative 5-year Recidivism of Released State Prisoners, 2005

Source: Durose, Cooper, and Snyder (2014), Bureau of Justice Statistics, Recidivism of Prisoners Released in 30 States in 2005;CEA Calculations.

Former Federal prisoners have relatively lower rates of recidivism; according to a recent study by the United States Sentencing Commission (USSC), about half of Federal prisoners released in 2005 were arrested again within 8 years and about a quarter returned to prison in this time frame

(USSC 2016). In this study, USSC also finds that criminal history is highly predictive of future offending, with re-offending rates after release decreasing for individuals that had fewer criminal history points and prior convictions before admission (Figure 22).[23]

Figure 22:
Cumulative 8-year Re-arrest of Released Federal
Prisoners by Criminal History Score, 2005

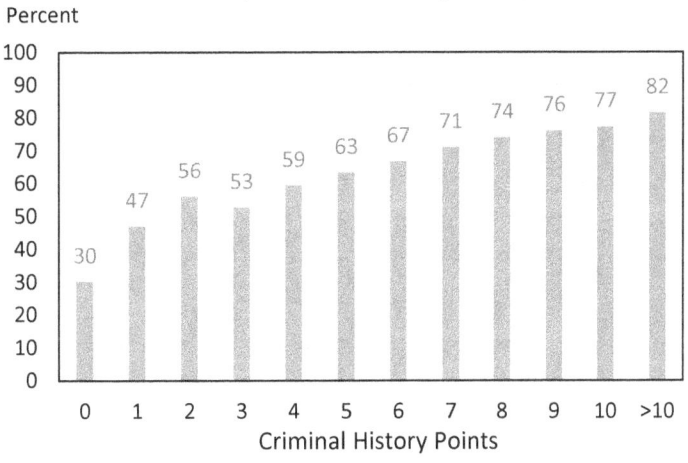

Source: United States Sentencing Commission, USSC (2016).

Demographics of the Incarcerated Population

The population that comes in contact with the criminal justice system is not representative of the U.S. population more broadly. Instead, the demographics of this group are highly concentrated, with an over-representation of Blacks and Hispanics, as well as low-income individuals. The incarcerated population also has a high prevalence of health and social risk factors, including mental illness, prior physical or sexual abuse, and drug and alcohol abuse.

The incarcerated population primarily consists of adult men. Though children below the age of majority (typically 18 years old) can be tried and detained as adults, most juveniles that are detained are held in designated facilities, such as detention centers, residential treatment centers, boot camps, and group homes. In recent decades, juvenile detention rates have declined, decreasing by over 50 percent between 1997 and 2013 (Figure 23). While the number of juveniles detained has declined, the age of majority is not uniform across states; in 10 states children under the age of 17 are tried as adults in criminal trials and face a higher risk of being sentenced to adult prison (Juvenile Justice Initiative 2016).

---

[23] Criminal history points are designations that reflect the number and severity of prior convictions. A higher number of criminal history points reflects a more significant criminal history.

27

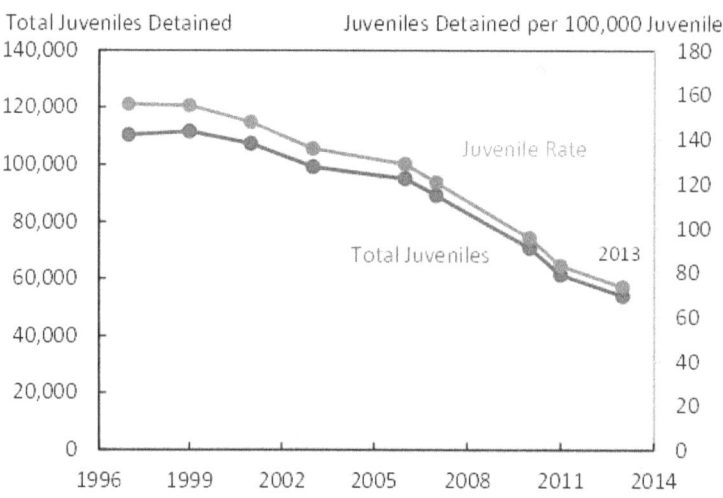

Figure 23:
Juvenile Detention, 1997-2013

Total Juveniles Detained   Juveniles Detained per 100,000 Juveniles

Source: Office of Juvenile Justice and Delinquency Prevention, Census, CEA Calculations.

Women comprise less than 10 percent of the total incarcerated population. Adjusting for population, female incarceration rates have increased faster than rates for men; since 1990, female incarceration rates have more than doubled, while male incarceration rates increased by 50 percent (Figure 24).

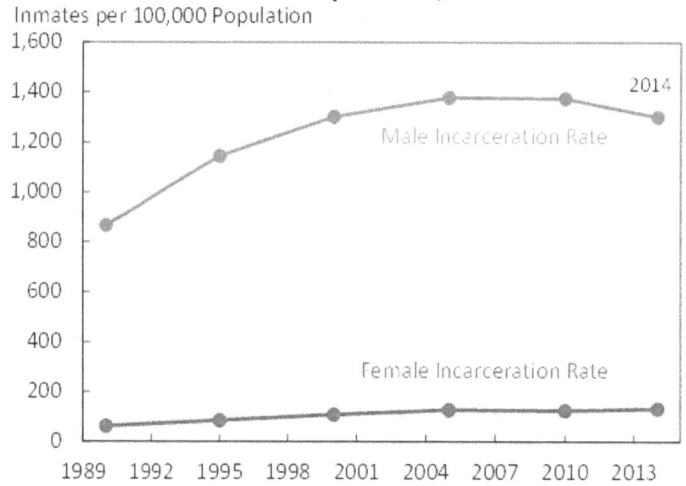

Figure 24:
Incarceration by Gender, 1990-2014

Inmates per 100,000 Population

Note: Rates include prison and jail inmates and are calculated within group.
Source: Bureau of Justice Statistics, Census, CEA Calculations.

Conversely, minority individuals are over-represented in the arrest and incarceration population. Total arrest rates for Blacks (per 100,000 residents) are double arrest rates for Whites. Though arrest rates have declined for all groups since 1990, current arrest rates still show marked disparities; in 2014, Black arrest rates were over 120 percent larger than the total arrest rate for all demographic groups (Figure 25). Racial disparities in drug arrests are particularly pronounced;

28

in 2014, drug arrest rates for Blacks were more than twice the drug arrest rates for Whites (UCR Arrest Data 2015, Census 2015, CEA Calculations). Though comprehensive data is not available for Native Americans over time, available evidence suggests that the arrest rate for Native Americans is 1.5 times the rate for Whites (Hartney and Vuong 2009).

Figure 25:
Arrest Rate Demographics, 1990-2014

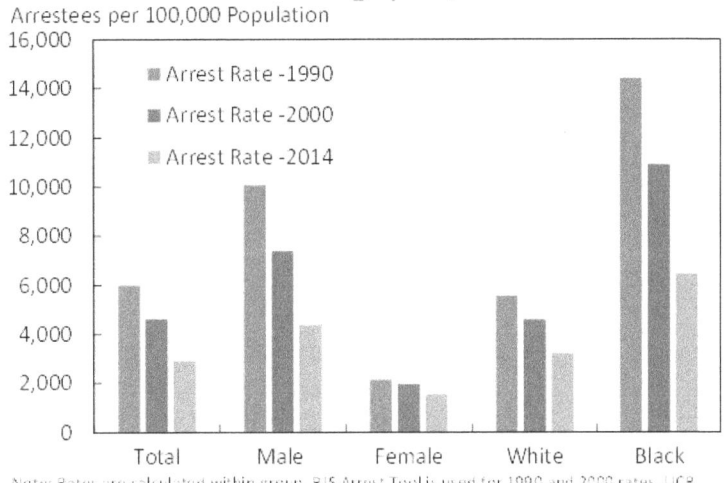

Note: Rates are calculated within group. BJS Arrest Tool is used for 1990 and 2000 rates, UCR data is used for 2014.
Source: FBI Uniform Crime Reports, Bureau of Justice Statistics, Census, CEA Calculations.

This pattern is also reflected in the incarcerated population. Though Blacks and Hispanics represent approximately 30 percent of the population, they comprise over half of those incarcerated (Census 2015; Carson 2015). While Black incarceration rates declined modestly between 2000 and 2014, the incarceration rate for Blacks dwarfs the rate of other groups, and is over 3.5 times larger than the rate for Whites (Figure 26). Descriptive statistics on arrests and incarceration partially reflect higher crime rates in minority communities; rigorous academic research, however, finds that racial disparities persist in police interactions, arrests, and sentencing, even after controlling for defendant and offense characteristics (Harris and Kearney 2014; Rehavi and Starr 2014; Truman and Langton 2015).

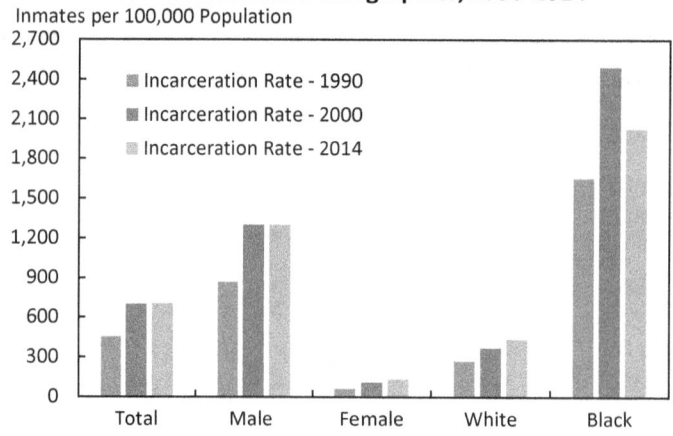

Figure 26:
Incarceration Rate Demographics, 1995-2014

Note: Rates include prison and jail inmates and are calculated within group.
Source: Bureau of Justice Statistics, Census, CEA Calculations.

A large body of literature in economics, sociology, psychology, and criminology finds that, for similar offenses, Blacks and Hispanics face a higher probability of arrest and conviction as well as harsher penalties. Controlled experiments reveal that implicit biases and stereotypes cause strong associations between minority individuals and criminal behavior, and these beliefs could impact decision-making in the criminal justice system and increase punishment severity for minorities (e.g. Eberhardt et al. 2004). While studies show that Blacks and Hispanics are no more likely to be found in possession of contraband than Whites, minority individuals are more likely than Whites to be stopped and searched, and these tactics contribute to higher rates of arrest for minority individuals (Anwar and Feng 2006; Antonovics and Knight 2009). Even after controlling for arrest offense and defendant characteristics, prosecutors are 75 percent more likely to charge Black defendants with offenses that carry mandatory minimums. Black defendants are 24 percent more likely to be convicted if their trial has a jury that was chosen from an all-white pool of eligible jurors, where eligibility is determined by random assignment of jury duty (Anwar, Bayer, and Hjalmarsson 2012). Following conviction, Black defendants receive longer sentences for similar offenses (Rehavi and Starr 2014). Given that minority defendants are more likely to have had contact with the criminal justice system than whites, they are also more likely to have a criminal record when charged with a new offense, and evidence of a criminal history increases the severity of any new punishment.

Figure 27:
Adults that Have Ever Been to Prison, 1974-2001

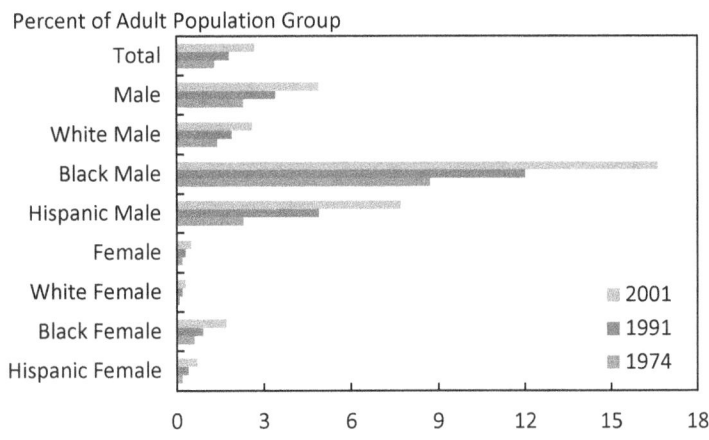

Source: Bonczar (2003), Bureau of Justice Statistics.

Along with rising incarceration rates, the share of the adult population that has a history of prior incarceration has also increased. Between 1974 and 2001, the proportion of the adult population that had ever been to prison more than doubled to 2.7 percent of the population. Over this period, the formerly imprisoned population increased for all demographic groups, with dramatic increases for Black and Hispanic men of 91 and 235 percent respectively. By 2001, 1 in 6 Black men had ever been to prison, up from 1 in 11 men in 1974. For women, overall rates were lower but racial disparities were comparable to those of men; in 2001, 1 in 200 women had a history of prior incarceration, but rates for Black women were more than 5.5 times the rate for White women (Figure 27).

Using estimates based on historical trends in imprisonment, nearly a third of Black males and one in six Hispanic males born in 2001 are expected serve time in prison in their lifetimes. The lifetime imprisonment rate for this cohort is estimated to be 5.5 times higher for Black men than White men. For women, 6 percent of Black women and 2 percent of Hispanic women born in 2001 are estimated to serve time in prison during their lifetimes, relative to 1 percent of White women (Figure 28).

Figure 28:

Projected Lifetime Chance of Serving Prison Time for Individuals Born in 1974-2001

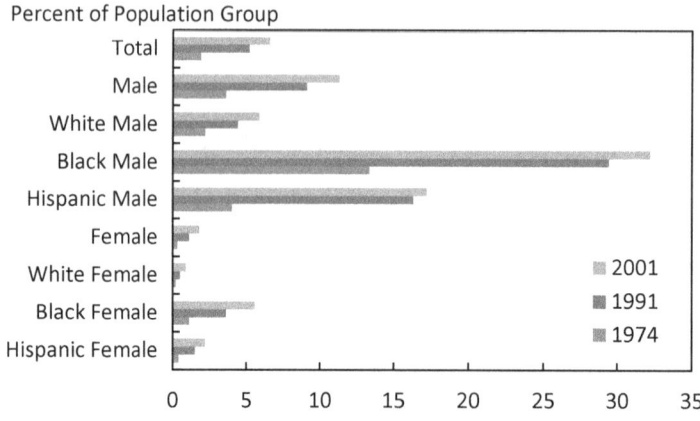

Note: Ever incarcerated rates for birth cohorts are based on 2001 projections that use the assumption that incarceration rates will follow 2001 trends in years following birth.
Source: Bonczar (2003), Bureau of Justice Statistics.

In addition to overrepresentation by minority groups, the incarcerated population is disproportionately poor with low levels of educational attainment. In this population, individuals are likely to have received public assistance, grown up in foster care, and experienced homelessness (Figure 29). Available data show that approximately 65 percent of prisoners did not complete high school and 14 percent have less than an 8th grade education, indicating that they may have limited earning ability and face a high rate of indigence (Harlow 2003).[24]

Figure 28 also shows rates of a number of other health and social risk factors in the incarcerated population. Substance abuse is a pervasive problem; 69 percent of the incarcerated population are regular drug users and 65 percent regularly use alcohol, while a third of prisoners and jail inmates had a parent that abused substances.[25] In addition, nearly a third of the incarcerated population has a family member that has also been incarcerated. The incarcerated population is also likely to experience traumatic abuse before entering custody; nearly 20 percent of prisoners and jail inmates have been physically or sexually abused prior to being incarcerated. Women involved in the justice system are more likely to have experienced traumatic abuse; over 50 percent of incarcerated women have been physically or sexually abused prior to incarceration (James and Glaze 2006).

---

[24] Of the proportion that have not completed high school, 28 percent of prisoners have a GED.

[25] Statistics for this figure combine reported rates of characteristics for individuals in James and Glaze (2006). James and Glaze (2006) provides rates split by mental health status and facility type (local jail, State prisons, and Federal prisons). The rates shown in this chart are constructed as weighted averages from these sub-categories, using the relative prevalence of mental health characteristics in each facility type and the proportion of the incarcerated population in each facility type. Jail statistics are derived from 2002 survey responses, while prison statistics come from a 2004 survey, and the total characteristic weighted averages account for this reporting year difference.

Figure 29:
Demographics of Incarcerated Population, 2002-2004

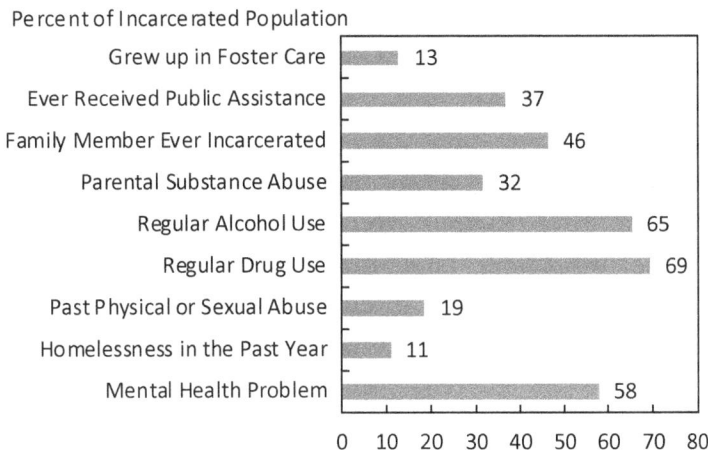

Percent of Incarcerated Population

Note: Statistics combine survey data from State and Federal prisoners in 2004 with Local Jail inmates in 2002.
Source: James and Glaze (2006), Bureau of Justice Statistics, CEA Calculations.

Lastly, over half of individuals with a history of incarceration also have mental health problems. In 2005, over half of the incarcerated population had a mental health problem, rates that greatly exceed the 11 percent of individuals with mental illness in the general population (James and Glaze 2006). More recent data from 2012 finds that 15 percent of prisoners and 26 percent of jail inmates suffer from serious psychological distress (Beck 2015).

Beginning in the 1950s, deinstitutionalization of mental health facilities in the United States has dramatically reduced the mental hospital inpatient population, which now is 5 times smaller than the population of mentally ill individuals behind bars. However, recent economic research suggests that transfers of the mentally ill from hospitals to prisons has played only a minor role in overall incarceration growth, causing a 4 to 7 percent increase in the incarcerated population (Raphael and Stoll 2013a).

Inmates with mental illness may be particularly vulnerable in a prison or jail setting; recent studies show that individuals with serious psychological distress were 2 to 8 percent more likely to be sexually victimized than other inmates while incarcerated (Beck et al. 2013). Mentally ill inmates are also 10-15 percent more likely to have issues with drug and alcohol abuse than inmates without mental health problems (James and Glaze 2006).

II. Costs and Benefits of Criminal Justice Policy from an Economic Perspective

From an economic perspective, the goal of an efficient criminal justice system is to maximize the safety of citizens and minimize criminal activity while also limiting the direct and indirect costs of criminal justice policies to individuals, communities and the economy.[26] Broadly, debates about the criminal justice system can be framed as a comparison of the system's societal benefits in terms of reduced crime and its societal costs in terms of direct government spending and collateral consequences for individuals, families and communities. Likewise, any reform should offer an improvement to current practice, through increasing safety, rebuilding communities, improving economic opportunity, or reducing expenditures or other social costs.

In this section, we review insights from economic research on crime and the criminal justice system and organize the discussion based on the broad benefits and costs of criminal justice policies. While criminal justice policies also raise many questions around humanitarian issues and social justice, we focus only on economic aspects to develop a cost-benefit framework based on economic research.

Costs of Crime to Victims and Society

The cost of crime is extensive, imposing burdens on victims, families and society. These costs include not only direct monetary losses, such as stolen or destroyed property or medical costs, but also other costs such as pain, suffering, trauma, fear, reduced quality of life or loss of life. Crime may also have indirect costs at the community level, including reduced business investment, lower property values, and declines in economic opportunity. Nonetheless, given the large reductions across categories of crime over the last two decades, current crime costs are lower than they have been historically.

The societal cost of crime in the United States likely totals hundreds of billions of dollars per year. In order to capture the value of direct and indirect costs of crime, researchers have used a number of approaches. These include itemized calculations (Miller, Cohen and Wiersema 1996; Anderson 1999), jury awards (Cohen 1988), contingent valuations of an individual's willingness to pay to avoid a crime (Cohen, Rust, Steen and Tidd 2004), and estimating the statistical value of life (Ashenfelter 2006). Given the variety of methods used and factors considered to evaluate crime costs, estimates vary substantially, as is shown in Table 1 below.

---

[26] Other goals of the criminal justice system include allowing for rehabilitation, expressing disapproval of certain kinds of behavior, providing consistent penalties across demographic groups, and punishing individuals appropriately for the crime committed.

Estimates of the Social Cost of Crime, 2014

Real (2015 $Billions)	Mean	Median	Min	Max
Cost of all Crimes by Category				
Murder	110.6	141.0	14.5	215.8
Rape	21.1	21.4	9.7	36.2
Assault	53.0	58.2	11.3	88.6
Robbery	56.0	25.9	4.2	140.9
Burglary	38.2	40.7	3.9	94.6
Larceny	23.1	5.9	2.2	63.5
Vehicle Theft	6.0	5.0	0.9	11.4
Implied Total Cost	307.9	298.0		

Note: Cost of crime estimates summarized for a sample of studies reviewed by CEA. Implied Total Costs are a lower bound of total crime costs, as they incorporate the costs of crime for the 7 FBI Index I crimes only. A number of studies calculate inclusive total cost figures rather than crime specific estimates (e.g. Anderson 1999). We do not include total cost studies because they are specific to crime rates in the time period of the study, crime specific cost studies allow for cost estimates to be translated to current crime patterns for a total cost estimate.

Source: FBI UCR crime data; CEA Calculations; Ashenfelter 2006; Cohen 1988; Cohen, Rust, Steen and Tidd 2004; Donohue 2009; McCollister, French, and Fang 2010; Miller, Cohen, Wiersema 1996; Mueller-Smith 2015; Viscusi 2000.

Criminal Justice Policies and Crime Reduction Benefits

A central goal of our criminal justice system is to maintain the safety of citizens. Research on the economics of crime has grown out of work by Gary Becker (1968) that conceptualizes criminal agents as rational actors, where each individual weighs the benefits of criminal activity against the costs of expected punishment and the availability of non-criminal outside options. Though criminal acts may often lack a "rational" basis, this framework proposes that crime may be reduced by decreasing the benefits associated with crime through altering criminal preferences, increasing the costs of crime by raising the likelihood and severity of punishment, or increasing the opportunity cost of crime by improving the outside options of potential offenders. In addition to these behavioral levers, incarceration can also reduce crime more directly by removing offenders from society and incapacitating individuals in prisons or jails.

In this section, we review economic research on the crime-reducing effects of police, criminal sanctions, and policies that improve alternatives to criminal activity through raising levels of employment, wages, and education.[27] This body of research finds that the crime reducing impact

---

[27] In this literature, crime outcomes are measured as either crimes that are reported to the police, crimes that are self-reported in surveys, or arrests. Most studies use crimes reported to police, both because this data is most comprehensive and may be more reliable than self-reports of criminal behavior. Arrests are also often used as crime outcomes, though arrests are not a direct reflection of crimes committed, because they are also a function of enforcement.

of increasing incarceration is lower than the benefits that accrue from investments in police, education, and jobs programs.

Incarceration and Crime Reduction

Criminal sanctions have the capacity to reduce crime through deterrence and incapacitation; however, marginal increases in incarceration may have small and declining benefits. [28] Despite a large expansion in the prison population over the last several decades, a large body of research has generally found that the aggregate impact of incarceration on crime is modest and that it declines as the prison population grows. Researchers who study crime and incarceration believe that the true impact of incarceration on crime reduction is small, with a 10 percent increase in incarceration decreasing crime by just 2 percent or less (Donohue 2009; Chalfin and McCrary 2014), though economic studies have found a range of estimates for the effect of incarceration on crime (e.g. Levitt 1996; Johnson and Raphael 2012).[29] One reason experts believe that the true crime-reducing impact of incarceration is small is that most studies do not account for individuals incarcerated in Federal prisons or local jails, which could lead to an over-estimate of the measured effect of incarceration (Donohue 2009).[30]

Additional incarceration may be particularly ineffective in reducing crime when incarceration rates are already high (Liedka, Piehl, and Useem 2006; Johnson and Raphael 2012). When incarceration rates are high, further incarceration entails incapacitating offenders who are on average lower risk, which means that their incarceration will yield fewer public safety benefits. Thus, given the size of the U.S. incarcerated population, the aggregate crime-reducing impact of increasing incarceration rates is likely to be minimal. In contrast, there is evidence that incarceration has larger effects on crime outside of the United States, and this may be due in part to lower incarceration rates abroad (e.g. Drago, Galbiati, and Vertova 2009; Bell, Jaitman, and Machin 2013).

---

[28] In practice, the effect of incarceration is difficult to measure because while incarceration may have the ability to reduce crime, areas with higher levels of crime also tend to have higher levels of incarceration, making it difficult to isolate the reduction effect when comparing crime and incarceration rates. This simultaneity or reverse causality issue is not just a problem in measuring the impact of incarceration, but also in measuring the impact of any criminal justice policy (such as police) that may be applied more heavily when crime rates rise. The research cited in this report uses careful empirical approaches that address this measurement challenge.

[29] Because of the simultaneity of incarceration and crime (as in policing), these studies have relied on using lags of incarceration, simulated instruments and other methods to estimate the impact of higher incarceration rates on crime.

[30] It is likely that States with high State prison populations may also have high local jail populations and a high number of Federal prisoners, meaning that State incarceration rates are positively related to Federal and local inmate populations. If this is the case, omitting Federal and local variation in incarceration will attribute greater reductions in crime to a State prison population that is lower than the true incarcerated population. This omitted variable bias could lead to overestimates of the capacity of incarceration to reduce crime in this literature. This critique may be applicable to other policy evaluations as well, leading to over-estimates of the impact of policies whenever they are positively correlated with other crime control activities that may not be controlled for in a study.

Research on the impact of sentence length has found that longer sentences are unlikely to deter prospective offenders or reduce targeted crime rates, and that incapacitation benefits decline as an individual ages in prison.[31] Strikingly, the threat of a longer sentence does not deter prospective youth offenders in the general population (Lee and McCrary 2005, 2009; Hjalmarsson 2009a). Lee and McCrary (2009) estimate juvenile arrest rates barely respond to increases in expected sentence length at the age of majority; they find that a 10 percent increase in average sentence length leads to a zero to 0.5 percent decrease in arrest rates.

A number of studies using state-level data find mixed evidence that repeat offender laws and sentence enhancements reduce crime (e.g. Kessler and Levitt 1999; Kovandzic 2001; Webster, Doob, and Zimring 2006). Using individual data, Helland and Tabarrok (2007) find that sentencing enhancements in California can reduce criminal activity through deterrence, but that the implementation costs of longer sentences likely outweigh their benefits.

At the same time, the incapacitation effects of a longer sentence depend on age and decline as an individual gets older (Sampson and Laub 2004; Blumstein and Nakamura 2009). Below Figure 30 shows that arrests peak in early adulthood and taper in middle age. The relationship between age and criminality suggests that incarceration has a smaller incapacitation benefit for older individuals.

---

[31] One challenge in the literature on sentencing policy is that it is difficult to disentangle the different channels through which sentences can affect crime. A treatment of a shorter sentence (relative to a longer sentence) means that an offender will not be incapacitated in the future, so criminal behavior after release can be interpreted as a "reverse" incapacitation effect.. At the same time, the experience of going to prison or serving a longer sentence can alter an individual's behavior after they are released, and this change in behavior can be interpreted as a recidivism effect.

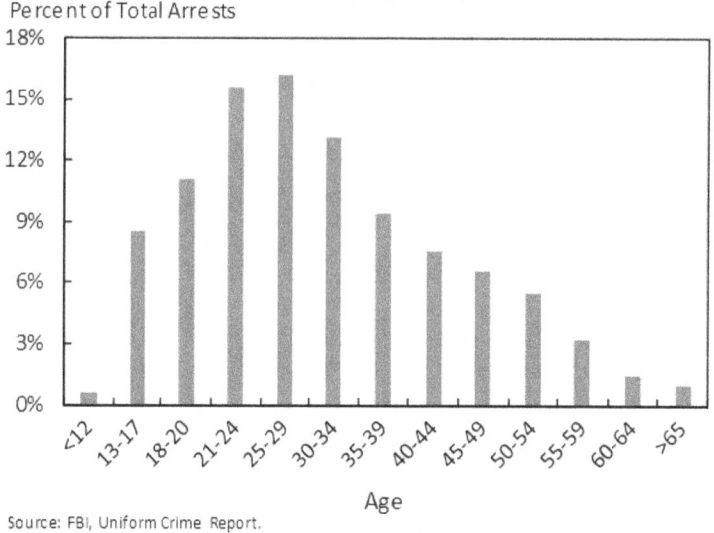

Figure 30:
Arrests by Age, 2014

Source: FBI, Uniform Crime Report.

Policies that adjust the certainty rather than the severity of punishment could have larger crime-reducing effects (Donohue 2009). A study by Hawken and Kleiman (2009) finds that probationers subject to frequent drug tests with immediate but brief incarceration penalties for violations were over 70 percent less likely to test positive for drugs than probationers subject to more infrequent drug tests with the threat of longer incarceration penalties.

More research is needed to understand the impact of other criminal sanctions, including monetary sanctions and probation. While some economists support the use of monetary sanctions as alternatives to harsher sanctions such as incarceration, the specific ways that these policies are implemented in the United States often renders them less effective and raises important humanitarian concerns, particularly that they unfairly disadvantage low-income offenders. In one of the few studies on monetary sanctions, Bar-Ilan and Sacerdote (2004) find that larger fines reduce traffic violations, though wealthier individuals are less responsive to changes in fine amounts, a finding that supports the use of fines that are equitable and proportional to income. Other researchers, typically focusing on uses of monetary sanctions internationally that differ substantially from U.S. policies, have argued that monetary sanctions could represent cost-effective alternatives to incarceration if they are executed equitably, with consideration for an offender's ability to pay, and if court administrators focus on strategies to improve fine collection (Piehl and Williams 2011). There is evidence, however, that monetary sanctions in the United States are inefficient tools to raise revenue and place a disproportionate burden on poor individuals (CEA 2015b).

In the United States, over 600,000 prisoners are released each year and over 70 percent of released prisoners are re-arrested within 5 years of release (Durose, Cooper, and Snyder 2014; Carson 2015). Because criminal offending has large societal costs, understanding the ways that particular penalties may affect re-offending is important to structuring criminal justice policy. Emerging research suggests that incarceration increases re-offending relative to alternative sanctions.

Incarceration could reduce re-offending if it serves to rehabilitate offenders, incapacitate the most active offenders, or if the experience of prison deters future criminal activity. Alternatively, incarceration could increase re-offending if it builds criminal expertise and limits post-release employment opportunities, either through skill atrophy or labor market stigma. Scholars in psychology and criminology have also proposed that incarceration could increase recidivism if it elevates an offender's feelings of resentment, strengthens personal identification as a delinquent, or creates social stigma that contributes to feelings of alienation (Matsueda 1992; Bernburg and Krohn 2003).

In line with these competing predictions, past research on the effect of incarceration on re-offending has found mixed results.[32] Studies in economics have sometimes found that incarceration and longer sentences could modestly reduce offending after release (Hjalmarsson 2009b). For example, an evaluation of a 2001 change in Maryland's sentencing guidelines found that an additional year incarcerated led to a decrease of 1.5 crimes per affected offender released (Owens 2009). In a second study using data from Georgia, Kuziemko (2013) finds that longer sentences are associated with lower re-offending rates, possibly due to the aging of inmates. However, she also finds that "truth-in-sentencing" laws, which limit opportunities for early parole release, significantly increase recidivism by dis-incentivizing inmates to exhibit model behavior and participate in rehabilitation programming, behaviors which would be rewarded in a parole system.

However, a growing body of work has found that incarceration increases recidivism. This research compares outcomes of defendants with similar characteristics and offenses and uses the random assignment of defendants to judges to predict a defendant's assigned sentence, based only on the judge's historical sentencing behavior. For instance, one recent study that uses highly detailed data from Texas uses this design and finds that although initial incarceration prevents crime through incapacitation, each additional sentence year causes an increase in future offending that eventually outweighs the incapacitation benefit. Each additional sentence year leads to a 4 to 7 percentage point increase in recidivism after release (Mueller-Smith 2015).

---

[32] Durlauf and Nagin (2011) note that research on the crime-reducing effects of sentencing laws may confuse impacts of recidivism, incapacitation and deterrence and this misinterpretation can overstate the positive impacts of longer sentences.

Similarly, a recent study exploiting random judge assignment in Chicago finds that juvenile detention increases the likelihood of re-offending after release by 22 to 26 percent and reduces the probability of earning a high school degree by 13 percent (Aizer and Doyle 2013). Using data on drug offenders in Washington D.C., another study found that incarceration may increase re-arrest rates relative to probation (Green and Winik 2010).[33]

These findings are consistent with research that finds that offenders build criminal connections while in residential facilities, and are more likely to recidivate given their exposure to other offenders (Chen and Shapiro 2007; Bayer, Hjalmarsson and Pozen 2009). Finally, there may be a psychological component to longer sentences; in a comparison of offenders that serve equal sentences, a 10 percent increase in sentence expectation increased recidivism by 1.2 percent (Bushway and Owens 2013).

Police and Crime Reduction

Police are a critical component of crime control and may reduce crime through deterrence, arrests, and building community trust. Economic research has consistently shown that police reduce crime in communities, and most estimates show that investments in police reduce crime more effectively than either increasing incarceration or sentence severity. Yet understanding how policing affects crime can be difficult because communities may react to rising crime levels by stepping up policing, making it difficult to separate cause from effect.[34] Several rigorous studies have addressed the problem of the joint determination of police and crime by measuring the crime-reducing impact of police hiring changes caused by external factors unrelated to local crime levels (e.g. Klick and Tabarrok 2005; Evans and Owens 2007; DeAngelo and Hansen 2014). This research shows that police reduce crime on average, and estimates of the impact of a 10 percent increase in police hiring lead to a crime decrease of approximately 3 to 10 percent, depending on the study and type of crime. Owens (2011) finds that larger police forces do not reduce crime through simply arresting more people and increasing incapacitation, instead, investments in police are likely to make communities safer through deterring crime.

There is also some evidence on the efficacy of various policing practices. For example, "hot-spots" policing, a strategy that intensifies policing in high crime locations within a city, may have the capacity to reduce crime with minimal displacement of crime to new areas (Braga, Papachristos and Hureau 2014). In contrast, research on "broken windows" policing, a strategy that focuses

---

[33] In this study, the authors found no statistical difference between the re-arrest rates of offenders that were incarcerated versus those that were sentenced to probation. However, because the authors begin measuring recidivism at the time of sentencing, individuals with prison terms have relatively less time in which they could be arrested and were arrested more in a shorter period of time after release.

[34] As with incarceration, simultaneity and reverse causality is an obstacle to measuring the impact of police on crime. The studies cited in this report address this measurement challenge using careful empirical approaches.

on high levels of enforcement for low-level crimes, has found generally weak crime-reducing effects (Harcourt and Ludwig 2007; Caetano and Maheshri 2013). A third category of policing strategies, "problem-oriented" policing, that approaches a particular crime problem through a combination of prevention, community outreach and engagement, has been more difficult to evaluate given a high level of variation across initiatives (Weisburd et al. 2010). Policing presence as well as specific policing strategies can increase the likelihood of apprehension for a given offense, and this increase in the certainty of punishment can deter individuals from engaging in criminal behavior in the first place (Nagin, Solow, and Lum 2015).

While research in economics finds substantial national effects of police hiring on crime reduction, it is important to emphasize that these average effects may not apply to specific jurisdictions. More research is needed to understand how to best improve the effectiveness of police and build constructive relationships between communities and law enforcement (Gill, Weisburd, and Telep 2016). Model policing tactics are marked by trust, transparency, and collaborations between police and community stakeholders, but more work is needed to identify and replicate best practices. Calls from citizens, policy-makers, and advocates to address issues related to police use of force, protection of constitutional rights, and police militarization stress the need to invest in policing strategies that both build trust and keep communities safe (Center for Constitutional Rights 2012; Kindy, Fisher, and Tate 2015; Dansky 2016). To further these goals, investments in police hiring should be accompanied with support for community policing and an emphasis on identifying effective policing strategies through evaluation.

Employment, Wage, and Education Policy, and Crime Reduction

Economic models of criminal behavior underscore another way that public policy can reduce crime: through establishing viable and meaningful alternatives to criminal behavior. Crime and poverty are correlated and criminal behavior is often motivated by a lack of economic opportunity. If legitimate employment opportunities with sufficient wages are available, then the necessity and relative attractiveness of criminal activity will decline. Likewise, investments in education can reduce crime by improving future labor market opportunities and by altering the propensity of children to engage in risky behaviors, even though they are not specifically designed to reduce crime. While a range of policies with different approaches, scalability, and implementation costs can be used to support employment, wage growth, and educational attainment, policies that constructively achieve these goals have large impacts on crime reduction.

To better understand the relationship between outside options and criminal activity, researchers have studied the effects of unemployment, business cycles and wages on crime. Declines in unemployment rates reduce crime levels, and crime is particularly sensitive to employment opportunities for low-skilled men (e.g. Raphael and Winter-Ebmer 2001; Ihlanfeldt 2007).

Similarly, evidence suggests that recessions can lead to cyclical increases in crime (Bushway, Cook, and Phillips 2010).

Wages measure the opportunity cost of crime more directly by quantifying the earnings an individual can obtain in the legal labor market, and studies have found that wage increases significantly decrease crime. Higher wages for low-skilled workers reduce both property and violent crime, as well as crime among adolescents (e.g. Grogger 1998; Doyle, Ahmed and Horn 1999). The impact of wages on crime is substantial; Gould, Weinberg, and Mustard (2002) estimate that a 10 percent increase in wages for non-college educated men results in approximately a 10 to 20 percent reduction in crime rates.[35]

Investments in education can reduce crime by expanding employment opportunities, and thereby improving non-crime alternatives. A number of studies have found that increases in compulsory schooling requirements reduce criminal activity by occupying students in school while they are adolescents (Anderson 2014) and by improving the long-term educational attainment and labor market outcomes of individuals (Lochner and Moretti 2004; Oreopoulos and Salvanes 2011).[36] The research on education and crime has found broad and meaningful effects; Lochner and Moretti (2004) estimate that a 10 percent increase in high school graduation rates results in 9 percent decline in criminal arrest rates.

Improvements in school quality can also have large returns in reducing criminal activity through both improving labor market outcomes and altering student behavior (Deming 2009a). For example, students who won school choice lotteries to attend high-achieving schools in Chicago were 60 percent less likely to report being arrested (Cullen, Jacob, and Levitt 2006). Likewise, reductions in school segregation have been shown to reduce crime in part by improving student outcomes (Weiner, Lutz, and Ludwig 2009).

Targeted education and jobs programs are also effective tools to prevent crime. By enhancing non-cognitive and behavioral skills and improving educational attainment, preschool education initiatives can have large crime-reducing effects (Heckman et al. 2010; CEA 2016). Interventions also have high returns for children and adolescents; for example, multiple evaluations have found

---

[35] As in studies of police and incarceration, it is difficult to identify a causal relationship between economic conditions and crime outcomes. The studies cited in this report do an excellent job of uncovering causal relationships through both panel data and instrumental variables techniques, which use external sources of variation to predict changes in economic conditions that are unlikely to be otherwise related to changes in crime rates. Examples include measuring changes in employment through changes in oil prices and prime defense contracts (Raphael and Winter-Ebmer 2001), and measuring changes in wages and employment through changes in industrial composition and technological change (Gould, Weinberg, and Mustard 2002).

[36] Research that measures the contemporaneous impact of increasing the number of required school days finds that daily schooling incapacitates property crime but increases violent crime, possibly through increasing negative peer interactions (Jacob and Lefgren 2003; Luallen 2006).

that an in-school cognitive behavioral therapy intervention for young men in Chicago significantly reduced arrests among participants (Heller et al. 2015). Lastly, summer youth employment can decrease criminal behavior of disadvantaged youth; a study of a summer jobs program in New York found that it reduced the probability of incarceration by 10 percent and decreased the mortality rates by 20 percent (Heller 2014; Gelber, Isen, and Kessler forthcoming).

Direct Government Spending on the Criminal Justice System

The U.S. criminal justice system is expansive in its goals, functions, and activities, and spans local, State, and Federal Government levels. Given the complex and interconnected structure of the criminal justice system, decomposing expenditures that correspond to particular initiatives is challenging. Though evaluation of specific policies is beyond the scope of this report, the broad discussion of criminal justice spending in this section provides motivation for reform opportunities that are capable of reducing costs while prioritizing safety.

Between 1993 and 2012, real total criminal justice spending increased by 74 percent, from $158 billion to $274 billion.[37] Approximately 50 percent of this spending is attributable to local governments, 30 percent is spent by States and 20 percent is spent by the Federal Government. Police are the largest outlay with real spending of $130 billion dollars in 2012, followed by $83 billion in corrections spending and approximately $60 billion in judicial and legal government spending (Figure 31).[38]

Figure 31:
Real Criminal Justice Expenditures by Type, 1993-2012

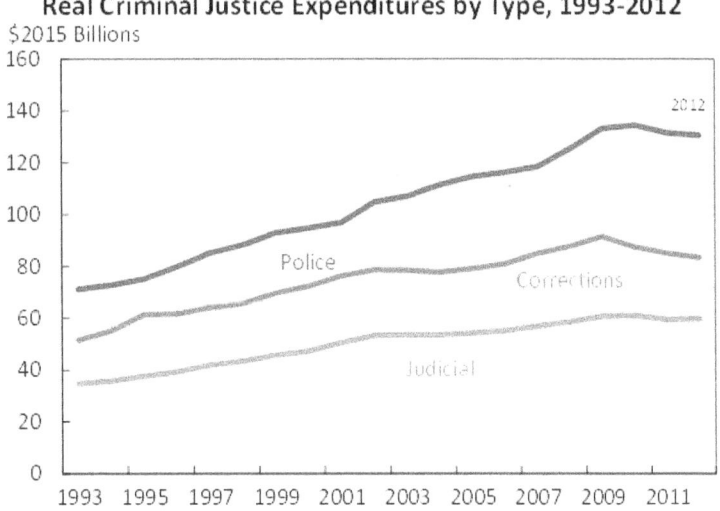

Note: Direct Expenditures in 2015 dollars included, intergovernmetnal transfers excluded.
Source: Bureau of Justice Statistics, 'Expenditure and Employment Extract' series.

---

[37] All dollar figures in this section are in 2015 dollars, adjusted using the CPI.

[38] Total criminal justice system expenditures do not include public spending on other categories of programs that may reduce crime, including funding for education and economic development. Bureau of Justice Statistics. 1993-2012. "Justice Expenditure and Employment Extracts" Series. Department of Justice, Washington, D.C.

On a per capita basis, real criminal justice spending was $872 dollars per person in the United States in 2012. Real per capita spending by States varies, with a high of $1,488, in Washington D.C. and a low of $407 in Indiana.[39] State corrections expenditures represent 7 percent of total State general funds on average, and 11 States spent more on corrections than on higher education in 2013 (Mitchell and Leachman 2014).

Recent survey data suggest that yearly average costs of confinement range from $14,000 to $60,000 per adult prisoner and $40,000 to $350,000 per juvenile detainee across States (Henrichson and Delaney 2012; Justice Policy Institute 2014). However, statistics on average costs mask the large fixed costs to building and operating a prison. Given that prisons are near capacity, adding additional prisoners may necessitate building additional facilities to avoid creating dangerous conditions of overcrowding. Given this environment, the direct cost of admitting a new prisoner likely exceeds any savings from releasing a prisoner. Expenditures for pretrial jail beds, a large portion of which are used for individuals unable to pay financial bail, are estimated to be $9 billion, or 11 percent of total spending on corrections (National Symposium on Pretrial Justice 2011).[40] In contrast to spending on incarceration, the average yearly salary expense per police officer was approximately $60,000 in 2014, similar to the yearly cost of a prison bed (Bureau of Labor Statistics 2016).

While spending on the court system has increased in recent decades, public resources for legal aid has waned, and lower levels of support for indigent defendants may contribute to the likelihood of incarceration. Between 1999 and 2007 public defender caseloads increased by 20 percent while staffing increased by only 4 percent, resulting in average caseloads of over 350 cases per defender per year (Langton and Farole 2010).[41] Despite the fact that over 5 million cases require indigent defense each year, States allocate only 10 percent of their judicial and legal budgets to legal aid, or approximately $2 billion annually (Langton and Farole 2010; Herberman and Kyckelhahn 2015).

These descriptive statistics do not imply that criminal justice spending is not justified or constructive. The demands and needs of criminal justice systems vary across States and cities within the United States. However, the large and increasing costs of the U.S. criminal justice system do show that enforcement has intensified over time and suggest that adjustments to current policy could provide real savings.

One way to benchmark indicators of criminal justice spending is to compare the United States to other countries. The United States had the largest prison population in the world, and an incarceration rate of approximately 700 prisoners per 100,000 residents, more than 4 times the world average in 2015 (Walmsley 2016). To accommodate the high rate of imprisonment, in

---

[39] *Ibid.*

[40] Pretrial bed estimate is referenced against 2012 spending figures. Bureau of Justice Statistics (BJS). 2012. "Justice Expenditure and Employment Extracts." Department of Justice, Washington, D.C.

[41] These statistics on public defenders are based on survey estimates for a subset of reporting states. Average caseload figures use statistics for all 50 states and the District of Columbia, while increases in caseloads and staffing are generalized from a sample of 17 states.

2007, the United States employed corrections officers at a rate over 2.5 times the world. At the same time, the United States employed over 30 percent fewer police officers per capita than other countries. With respect to judicial personnel, the United States' employment rates of prosecutors and judges are close to rates around the world (Figure 32; Harrendorf, Heiskanen and Malby 2010).

Figure 32:
Percent Difference in U.S. Rate Relative to Average of the World

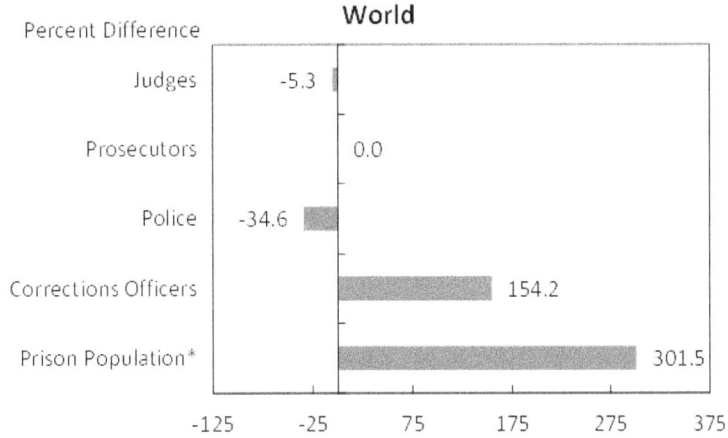

Note: World averages are for over 200 countries and territories. All outcomes are from 2007 except the prison population which uses data from 2015. Rates are per 100,000 residents.
Source: UN Crime Statistics, World Prison Population List.

Collateral Consequences of the Criminal Justice System

The costs of criminal justice policies are not limited to direct government expenditures. Individuals who obtain a criminal record or serve a prison sentence often face difficult circumstances when they return to society. Having a criminal record or a history of incarceration is a barrier to success in the labor market, and limited employment or depressed wages can stifle an individual's ability to become self-sufficient. Beyond earnings, criminal sanctions can have negative consequences for individual health, debt, transportation, housing, and food security. Further, criminal sanctions create financial and emotional stresses that destabilize marriages and have adverse consequences for children. Lastly, at the community level, collateral consequences exacerbate inequality and can deteriorate trust in government.

Collateral Consequences in the Labor Market

An estimated 70 million Americans—or roughly a third of the adult population—have some type of criminal record, and criminal records limit employment options in many industries and occupations (Bureau of Justice Statistics 2012; Rodriguez and Emsellem 2011; Vallas and Deitrich 2015).[42] Recent surveys find that over 70 percent of employers conduct criminal background checks, roughly double the rate during the 1990s (Holzer, Raphael and Stoll, 2006; Society for

---

[42] This group includes those with charges that were dismissed or did not result in conviction, as well as those who have completed their legal obligation to serve time in incarceration.

Human Resource Management 2012). Individuals with criminal records are frequently barred from obtaining occupational licenses; according to the American Bar Association, there are over 1,000 mandatory license exclusions for individuals with records of misdemeanors and nearly 3,000 exclusions for felony records (American Bar Association 2016).[43]

Employers could prefer not to hire individuals with records because they may perceive prior offenses as a predictor of lower productivity, dishonesty, or future criminality. Additionally, employers may be liable for criminal actions committed by employees through negligent hiring law suits (Raphael 2011). However, research suggests that employers who avoid applicants with criminal records overestimate the link between criminal histories and workplace productivity or the propensity to reoffend (Kurlychek, Brame, and Bushway 2007; Roberts et al. 2007; Blumstein and Nakamura 2009). Further, expanding the applicant pool available to employers could increase the quality of job matches, or the fit of an applicant's skills to the employer's needs, improving the productivity and profits of firms.

Because the incarcerated population is disproportionately poor and has low education levels, on average, labor market attachment is likely low for this group, even prior to conviction. Estimates from different data sources suggest that as little as 10 percent of this group have positive pre-incarceration earnings and that real pre-incarceration yearly earnings range from $3,000 to $28,000 (James and Glaze 2006; Kling 2006; Sabol 2007; Donohue 2009). Time spent incarcerated results in a loss of any earnings, and this puts additional strain on families that already have limited resources. A recent paper suggests that the probability that a family is in poverty increases by 38 percent while a father is incarcerated (Johnson 2009).

The negative employment and wage effects of labor market stigma extend beyond the formerly incarcerated population to the broader group of individuals with criminal records (Raphael 2011). Analysis that compares individual earnings before and after an arrest suggests that arrests can decrease earnings and employment (Grogger 1995). Furthermore, in a recent audit experiment, researchers randomly assigned a criminal record to otherwise identical job applications and found that applicants with criminal records were 50 percent less likely to receive an interview request or job offer, and differences were larger for Black applicants (Figure 33; Pager 2003; Pager, Western, and Sugie 2009).

---

[43] Beyond their implications for individuals with criminal records, occupational licensing policies also affect workers' access to jobs more generally, their wages, and their ability to move across State lines, as well as consumers' access to goods and services. More than one-quarter of U.S. workers require a license to do their jobs (CEA et al. 2015).

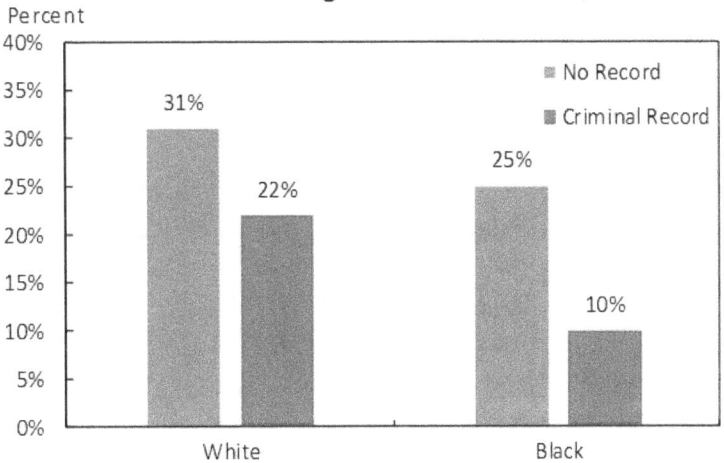

Figure 33:
Interview Call-backs given Criminal Record, 2004

Note: Call-back rates are from a randomized audit experiment that varied race and criminal record on otherwise identical job applications.
Source: Pager, Western, and Sugie (2009).

Likewise, research suggests that there are material labor market consequences to having any spell of incarceration (Nagin and Waldfogel 1998; Western 2002). Even after controlling for a broad range of characteristics like education and demographics, the formerly incarcerated earn substantially less than other workers—on the order of 10 to 40 percent less (Geller, Garfinkel, and Western 2006; The Pew Charitable Trusts 2010). Additionally, States with more flexible labor market conditions for individuals with criminal records may have lower recidivism rates (Hall, Harger and Stansel 2015).

Longer incarceration sentences may also be associated with greater skill loss and higher costs to re-integrating in the labor market, though these costs may be partially offset by participation in rehabilitation or correctional education programs (Kling 2006; Landersø 2015). A recent paper using variation in random judge assignment in Texas finds large negative impacts of sentence length on employment; in this setting, a one year increase in sentence length reduces employment by 4 percentage points and reduces earnings by approximately 30 percent after release (Mueller-Smith 2015). Individuals that cannot find sustainable employment given labor market barriers to reentry may also have a higher risk of re-offending.

Because Blacks are more likely to be incarcerated than Whites, the labor market consequences of conviction have broader implications for income inequality across demographic groups. The high rate of Black incarceration has contributed to lower labor force participation among Blacks and slower average wage growth relative to Whites (Grogger 1992; Holzer, Offner, and Sorenson 2005; Neal and Rick 2014). While the Black-White wage gap converged by 13 percent between 1950 and 1990 for employed men, accounting for non-employed men, including those incarcerated, reduces these gains to only 3 percent (Chandra 2000). Incarceration has been a key driver of growth in the population of non-employed Black men; in 1980, 11 percent of non-employed Black men were incarcerated but by 1999, this proportion had risen to 33 percent (Western and Pettit 2005).

The collateral consequences of criminal sanctions are not limited to employment, and can include negative impacts on health, debt, transportation, housing, and food security. These impacts amount to serious disadvantages for individuals with criminal records or a history of incarceration.

Incarcerated individuals face substantial health risks. When prisons are at capacity or overcrowded, the risk of inmate injury, sexual victimization, disease transmission and death can increase. A recent study finds that court orders to reduce crowding in State prisons led, on average, to a reduction of six prisoner deaths per year (Boylan and Mocan 2013). Harsh prison conditions are not limited to crowding, so-called "supermax" incarceration and solitary confinement have been linked to a range of mental health conditions, violent behaviors, and increased recidivism (Haney 2003; Lovell, Johnson, and Cain 2007; Mears and Bales 2009). These combined health risks lead to health worse health outcomes for the formerly incarcerated later in life (Massoglia 2008).

Inmates in prisons and jails are also much more likely to be sexually victimized; 3.7 percent of men and 8.5 percent of women experience sexual abuse while incarcerated, high rates compared to estimates of annual sexual assault incidence in the general population of 0.0001 percent of men and 0.004 percent of women (Beck et al. 2013; Planty et al. 2013). Though many sexual abuse incidents in prisons involve other inmates as perpetrators, over half of reported sexual victimizations are perpetrated by prison and jail staff (Beck et al. 2013). Beyond raising humanitarian concerns, harsh prison conditions do not deter individuals from offending after release (Chen and Shapiro 2007).

Meanwhile, monetary penalties and financial bail can create and exacerbate financial hardship. Monetary penalties include fines, which are punishments for an offense, and fees, which are itemized payments for criminal justice functions charged after a conviction. These sanctions can apply to individuals with even minor offenses, like traffic tickets (CEA 2015b). Tens of millions of individuals in the United States have been assessed fines or fees and the use of monetary sanctions has increased substantially over time, despite the fact that the collection of criminal justice debt is often inefficient (Beckett and Harris 2011). Individuals can also be subject to flat surcharges for collecting monetary penalties that range from $25 to $500 dollars as well as high interest rates and processing fees of up to 40 percent (Beckett, Harris, and Evans 2008; Diller 2010). Because monetary sanctions are typically assigned without consideration for an individual's ability to pay, these penalties can create onerous debt and obstacles to reentry for poor individuals. In some cases, a failure to pay fines and fees can even result in jail time (Diller, Greene, and Jacobs 2009).

Concurrent with the increase in fines and fees, available data suggests that the use of bail bonds has also increased by more than 130 percent over the past two decades.[44] Even relatively low bail payments generate substantial obstacles for poor defendants, and financial bail policies often detain the poorest rather than the most dangerous defendants (Baradaran and McIntyre 2012). In New York City in 2010, approximately 80 percent of defendants could not make bail at amounts less than $500 (Phillips 2012). Though the majority of bail payments are returned to defendants upon appearing in court, patching together funds to post bail or pay a bail bondsman can create significant financial hardship for families, as fees for using bail bondsmen can exceed 10 percent (Neal 2012).

Having a criminal record can also directly affect housing security after release. Though the U.S. Department of Housing and Urban Development (HUD) does not have a blanket prohibition of individuals with criminal records residing in public housing, in practice, each local Public Housing Authority (PHA) has the latitude to set its own criminal record policies (HUD 2015). Though restrictions vary by PHA, they are almost always more strict than Federal guidelines, often barring individuals with criminal records from obtaining housing assistance. Individuals with limited resources and few housing options may be denied public housing assistance for low-level nonviolent offenses, including prior alcohol and drug use (Curtis, Garlington, and Schottenfeld 2013). In some cases, housing restrictions for individuals with criminal records can ultimately lead to homelessness (Rodriguez and Brown 2003). Reentry barriers contribute to low housing security after prison; the average parolee in Michigan moved 2.6 times in the two years following prison (Harding, Morenoff, and Herbert 2013). Individuals with a history of mental illness and addiction face greater challenges in housing security; research on released prisoners in Boston finds that this population was up to 50 percent more likely to have temporary or marginal housing 6 months after release (Western et al. 2014).

Beyond restrictions to housing assistance, a criminal record also restricts access to important safety net programs that provide much-needed support for lower-income individuals, including food stamps (Supplemental Nutrition Assistance (SNAP)) and welfare assistance (Temporary Assistance for Needy Families (TANF)) under Federal law. Though many States have overridden Federal restrictions to allow access to these benefits, individuals with a felony drug record are fully or partially excluded from SNAP benefits in 30 States and TANF benefits in 36 States (Beitsch 2015). For poor individuals, these restrictions can create reentry barriers to obtaining the most basic necessities.

In jurisdictions across the United States, a number of offenses and infractions can also result in the loss of a driver's license, and this loss of transportation may make it difficult to maintain employment. Though most driver's license suspensions and revocations result from driving offenses, the American Bar Association estimates that 181 State rules and statutes suspend or revoke a driver's license for a non-driving offense (American Bar Association 2016). In 46 States, an individual's driver's license may be revoked for failure to comply with a child support order,

---

[44] Bureau of Justice Statistics. 1990-2009. "Felony Defendants in Large Urban Counties" Series. Department of Justice, Washington, D.C.

which may result from a lack of resources (FindLaw 2016). Furthermore, losing a driver's license may also be used as a penalty for failure to pay criminal justice debt (Bannon, Nagrecha, and Diller 2010).

Collateral Consequences for Families, Communities, and Minority Groups

The collateral consequences of criminal sanctions are not limited to individuals, but can have ramifications for families and communities. Obstacles in the labor market for individuals with a criminal record can put a strain on family resources and contribute to broader income inequality. Meanwhile, the stresses of incarceration can increase the likelihood of divorce and have negative impacts on children.

Because incarceration secludes individuals from their families and communities, it decreases the likelihood of marriage and increase the likelihood of divorce. Young offenders face lower odds of marrying while incarcerated, potentially permanently decreasing their likelihood of marrying and forming a family (Raphael 2006a). Likewise, prolonged separation between spouses while a husband or wife is incarcerated increases the likelihood of divorce (Massoglia, Remster, and King 2011).

Parental incarceration likely has high costs to children. More than 5 million children have a parent who is currently incarcerated or has been incarcerated in the past (Murphey and Cooper 2015). Over half of all prisoners are parents, and the number of parents in prisons has increased sharply along with the overall rise in incarceration. The rise in imprisonment of parents has proportionally increased the number of children with a parent in prison; in 2007, the Bureau of Justice Statistics estimated that 1.7 million children had a parent in prison, though other research estimates are as high as 2.7 million children (Figure 34; Glaze and Maruschak 2008; The Pew Charitable Trusts 2010). In a reflection of the demographics of the incarcerated population, 1 percent of White children have a parent in prison compared to 7 percent of Black children and 2 percent of Hispanic children (Glaze and Maruschak 2008). Furthermore, it appears that the incidence of parental incarceration may fall more heavily on those imprisoned for relatively lower risk and nonviolent crimes. By offense category, individuals imprisoned for non-violent drug crimes or public order crimes are 20 percent more likely to be parents than individuals in prison for violent or property crimes (Glaze and Maruschak 2008).

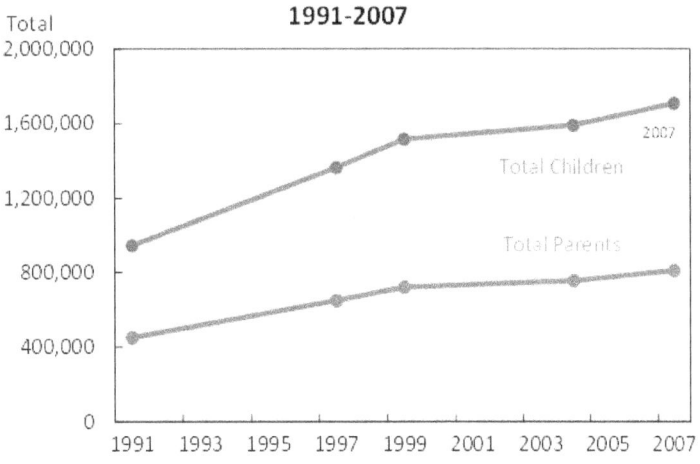

Figure 34:
Number of Parents in Prison and their Minor Children, 1991-2007

Source: Bureau of Justice Statistics Special Report, Glaze and Maruschak (2008).

Parental incarceration is a strong risk factor for a number of adverse outcomes, including antisocial and violent behavior, mental health problems, school dropout, and unemployment (Murray and Farrington 2008). In its 2012 report to the Attorney General, the National Task Force on Children Exposed to Violence found that traumatic events, including parental arrest and incarceration increases the risk of post-traumatic stress disorder in children (Listenbee et al. 2012). Researchers have found that these effects extend to child behavior outcomes; Wildeman (2010), for instance, finds that paternal incarceration is associated with higher levels of physical aggression among boys as young as five years old. Similarly, Johnson (2009) finds that parental incarceration is associated with behavioral problems in children, and that these effects are largest if the parent is incarcerated while the child is a teenager. Finally, a recent paper using Swedish data finds that children of fathers who have been incarcerated are more likely to be incarcerated themselves. They find that the intergenerational transmission of crime may be partly explained by differences in parental education and parenting behaviors (Hjalmarsson and Lindquist 2012).

In addition to impacts on families, the collateral consequences of the criminal justice system are concentrated in poor and minority communities, and this has implications for economic and social inequality. Moreover, the outsized involvement of poor and minority residents in the criminal justice system can magnify collateral consequences at the community level and contribute to distrust in government. In neighborhoods that are primarily poor and have high proportions of minority residents, collateral consequences for individual employment, family stability and child well-being can compound other economic disadvantages and deteriorate community trust in government and the criminal justice system. In recent years, high-profile protests in response to police use of force in Ferguson, Cleveland, New York, and Baltimore provide evidence that communities are frustrated with many aspects of the criminal justice system (Kang 2015). Relative to Whites, Blacks and Hispanics that reported being stopped by police in street or traffic stops were significantly less likely to view the stop as legitimate (Langton and DuRose 2013).

Costs and Benefits of Criminal Justice Policies

Weighing the costs and benefits of criminal justice policy is context-specific, and depends on the population affected and the reform alternatives available. The benefits of criminal justice policies include the potential to increase safety and minimize the direct and indirect cost of crime, while the costs of policies include direct government expenditures and the collateral consequences of criminal sanctions.

Several economists have performed formal cost-benefit calculations of criminal justice policies. Given the small size of the marginal impact of incarceration on crime, most cost-benefit calculations find that the costs of incarceration and sentencing policy outweigh the benefits in the United States, even though many of these calculations do not consider the added indirect costs related to collateral consequences. In contrast, several economic studies have determined that investments in police and education are cost-effective and have large net benefits. Table 2 summarizes the findings of cost-benefit analyses of U.S. criminal justice policies, separated by policy area.

Table 2:

**Tally of Cost-Benefit Analyses of Criminal Justice Policy:
Evidence from Economics Literature**

		Percent of Studies	
	Number of Studies	Consider Indirect or Collateral Consequences	Cost-Effective Policy
Police	6	17%	83%
Incarceration	7	43%	29%
Sentencing	5	40%	20%
Education	9	67%	100%

Note: Estimates are derived from economics studies that focus on the United States and conduct cost-benefit analyses. The studies differ in policy setting, outcomes, time frame and methodological approaches. Conclusions about the cost-effectiveness of policies are taken from the analysis and expertise of the authors in each study.

Sources: Police: Levitt 1997; Cohen and Ludwig 2003; Evans and Owens 2007; Caetano and Maheshri 2013; Chalfin and McCrary 2013; DeAngelo and Hansen 2014.
Incarceration: Levitt 1996; Spelman 2000; Kuziemko and Levitt 2004; Spelman 2005; Donohue 2009; Hjalmarsson 2009b; Lofstrom and Raphael 2013.
Sentencing: Owens 2009; Helland and Tabarrok 2007; Iyengar 2008; Kuziemko 2013; Mueller-Smith 2015.
Education: Donohue and Siegelman 1998; Reynolds et al. 2001; Lochner, 2004; Lochner and Moretti 2004; Schweinhart et al. 2005; Belfield et al. 2006; CPPRG 2007; Deming 2009b; Oreopoulos and Salvanes 2011; Anderson 2014.

Cost-benefit analyses of incarceration weigh the direct costs of incarcerating an individual against the social value of crimes that may have been averted due to incarceration. Lofstrom and Raphael (2013) examine a 2011 policy change in California that resulted in the realignment of 27,000 State prisoners to county jails or parole. They find that realignment had no impact on violent crime, but that an additional year of incarceration is associated with a decrease of 1 to 2 property crimes, with effects strongest for motor vehicle theft. Applying estimates of the societal cost of crime, the authors calculate that while the cost of a year of incarceration is $51,889 per prisoner in California, the societal value of the corresponding reduction in motor vehicle thefts is only $11,783, yielding a loss of $40,106 per prisoner. Notably, this net loss per prisoner would be larger if the study considered the additional costs of collateral consequences, such as lost earnings or potential increases in re-offending due to incarceration. These estimates highlight the fact that there are more cost-effective ways of reducing crime than incarceration, such as investing in law enforcement, education, and policies that expand economic opportunity.

In contrast to studies of incarceration and sentencing, research shows that investments in police have high returns. In a study of the impact of a mass layoff of highway troopers in Oregon, DeAngelo and Hansen (2014) found that traffic fatalities and non-fatal injuries significantly increased, due to a greater prevalence of dangerous driving and drunk driving. The estimates in this paper suggest that the state trooper salary cost required to save a life is $309,000, which is very low compared to estimates of the statistical value of life, which range from $1 million to $10 million (e.g. Viscusi 2000; Cohen et al. 2004).

Similarly, the cost-effectiveness of education as an intervention to reduce crime is clear. Lochner and Moretti (2004) conduct a cost-benefit analysis of the effect of increasing the high school graduation rate on crime and arrest rates. Comparing costs and benefits in 1990, they estimate that while the yearly per pupil cost of secondary school is $6,000, the societal benefit from reducing crime is $1,170-$2,100 per additional male graduate, including reductions in victim costs, property damages, and incarceration costs. When these benefits are considered alongside an $8,040 increase in annual income from a high school degree, the benefits of an additional high school graduate are tremendous, amounting to over $160,000 in discounted value per graduate (Lochner and Moretti 2004; CEA Calculations).[45] In aggregate, the authors calculate that a 1 percent increase in the total high school graduation rate generates a $1.4 billion benefit due to reductions in crime rates.

The cost-effectiveness of a policy also depends on the population affected. For the most part, economic studies of the impacts of criminal justice policies have focused on the total average effect of a policy across all types of individuals and offenses. However, the direct costs and collateral consequences of incarceration are likely more important for low-risk offenders, a group which may include non-violent drug offenders and older offenders that have already served long sentences.

---

[45] This calculation assumes a 30 year work career per graduate and a discount rate of 3 percent.

Applying an economic lens is not the only tool available to evaluate the criminal justice system, but it can be a useful one. The evidence reviewed in this section highlights the substantial costs of current criminal justice policies and a strong body of research finding that the costs of several criminal justice policies likely outweigh their benefits. While research provides mixed evidence on whether incarceration deters crime, it offers unanimous findings that alternative policies like increasing educational attainment or the number of police effectively decrease crime rates. These policies typically have a much larger impact and can provide a more cost-effective approach without the negative humanitarian costs of incarceration policies. Criminal justice policies retain an important role in promoting public safety; however, the substantial research reviewed in this section suggests that current criminal justice policies need reform.

To weigh the relative crime-reducing benefits of different policies, CEA conducted a "back-of-the-envelope" cost-benefit analysis of three policies: increasing the prison population, expanding the police force, and raising the minimum wage. In each calculation, CEA considered only the relative potential of these policies to reduce crime and did not consider their impacts on other outcomes. In the case of incarceration, for example, collateral consequences would further reduce the total benefits of this policy relative to the estimates below.

In assessing each of these policy changes we bound the policy's impact on crime drawing on estimates from leading studies. We then translate these crime reductions into dollars using estimates of the social cost of crime from the economics literature. For the social cost of crime, we use a central estimate from the literature of $33,000 per crime, which subsumes the varying costs of different types of crime but facilitates straightforward and transparent calculations.[1]

For incarceration and police, CEA considered the impact of spending an additional $10 billion dollars per year on each policy, which translates to a 12 percent increase in corrections spending and an 8 percent increase in police spending. We then assume that additional spending is devoted entirely to increasing the incarcerated population and police hiring, respectively. Applying crime reduction effects and social cost of crime estimates from the economics literature, we find that a $10 billion dollar increase in incarceration would decrease crime rates by 1 to 4 percent (or 55,000 to 340,000 crimes annually) and lead to a societal benefit ranging from −$8 billion to $1 billion—although as noted the societal benefits are likely somewhat lower because these numbers do not include collateral consequences of incarceration like its effects on future earnings of prisoners or their families. The same spending on police would decrease crime rates by 5 to 16 percent (or 440,000 to 1.5 million crimes annually) and lead to a societal benefit of $4 billion to $38 billion (Figure 35).[2]

Figure 35:

Estimated Societal Benefit of a $10 Billion Increase in Spending, Incarceration vs. Police

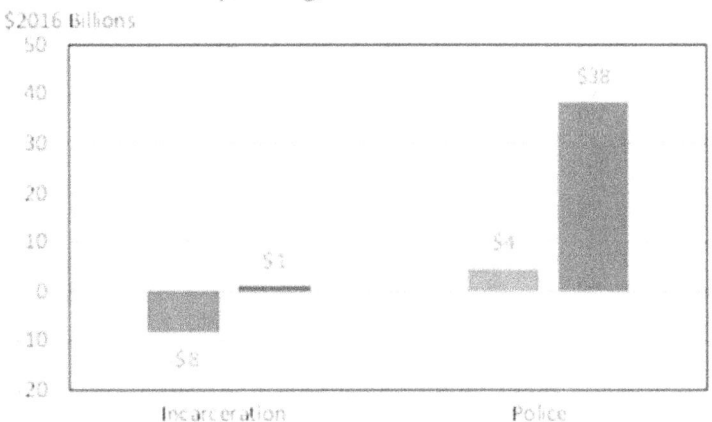

Source: Bureau of Justice Statistics, FBI UCR, BLS, CEA Calculations

Next, we consider the impact of increasing the minimum wage to $12 an hour by 2020. As discussed above, wage increases can reduce crime by providing viable and sustainable employment alternatives to criminal activity. Using estimates from Gould, Weinberg, and Mustard (2002) that relate crime to changes in wages for non-college educated men, we find that increasing the minimum wage to $12 per hour would decrease crime rates by 3 to 5 percent (or 250,000 to 510,000 crimes annually) and lead to a societal benefit of $8 billion to $17 billion (Figure 36).[3]

Figure 36:

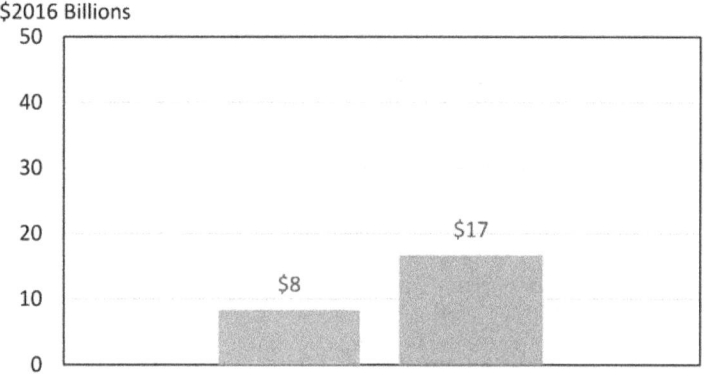

Estimated Societal Benefit of a $12 Minimum Wage by 2020 due to Crime Reduction

Note: Analysis considers the effect of a 2020 increase to $12 an hour in current dollars or deflated to current nominal dollars.
Source: Bureau of Justice Statistics, FBI UCR, BLS, Gould, Weinberg, and Mustard (2002); CEA Calculations

---

[1] The societal cost of crime estimate is drawn from literature described in Table 1.

[2] The impact on crime of spending additional resources on policing or incarceration was determined by applying conservative estimates from high quality studies. Because the impacts of policing and incarceration tend to vary by crime, we use the lowest and highest estimates across crimes for each policy change to bound the potential effect. Estimates of the crime reduction effects of a one percent increase in the incarcerated population range from a 0.05 to 0.3 percent and for policing range from 0.3 to 1 percent. As $10 billion of increased spending translates into 12 percent more spending on incarceration and 8 percent more spending on policing, such spending increases would reduce crime by 1 to 4 percent (56,614 to 339,685 crimes) and 5 to 16 percent (442,843 to 1,476,143 crimes), respectively. Given a social cost of crime of $32,729, we determine that $10 billion dollars in additional incarceration spending would yield social benefits of -$8 billion to $1 billion, while the same amount of spending on police hiring would yield social benefits of $4 billion to $38 billion.
The incarceration elasticity range used draws on the following studies: Spelman 2000, 2005; Liedka, Piehl, and Useem 2006; Donohue 2009; Johnson and Raphael 2012; Chalfin and McCrary 2014.
The police elasticity range used draws on the following studies: McCrary 2002; Klick and Tabarrok 2005; Evans and Owens 2007; Lin 2009; Shi 2009; Chalfin and McCrary 2013, 2014; DeAngelo and Hansen 2014.

[3] The impact of a minimum wage increase on the wages of non-college educated men was determined using wage data from the March Current Population Survey and deflating a 2020 minimum wage of $12 back to 2016 dollars using the Consumer Price Index. The impact of crime was determined using a range of elasticities of -1 to -2 relating wages for non-college educated men to reductions in crime, drawn from Gould, Weinberg, and Mustard (2002). These estimates translate to an estimated reduction in crime by 3 to 5 percent (254,967 to 509,933 crimes) given the 3 percent increase in average wages for non-college educated men that would result from this minimum wage increase. We assume such a minimum wage increase would have no employment impacts, with an employment elasticity of 0.1 the benefits would be somewhat lower.

III.   Taking the Next Step: Promising Areas for Reform and Administration Action

Acting on a strong body of research demonstrating the negative impacts of our current criminal justice policies and more effective alternatives, President Obama has advocated evidence-based criminal justice reform that works to ameliorate the long-term causes of crime, improve public safety at present, and help those with criminal justice involvement re-integrate into their communities. The 2017 Budget proposes the 21st Century Justice Initiative, a $5 billion investment of $500 million per year over 10 years. The Initiative will focus on reducing crime, reversing practices that have led to unnecessarily long sentences and unnecessary incarceration, and building community trust. President Obama has laid out the three key areas for reform: the community, the courtroom, and the cell block. Community reforms such as investments in education can reduce involvement with the criminal justice system, while community policing and enhanced police transparency can improve community safety and build trust. Changing employment restrictions and improving access to health care and housing can reduce the collateral consequences of convictions. The President's broader economic strategy that is aimed at promoting growth, and raising wages and incomes, also helps to reduce crime through providing viable economic alternatives to criminal activity. Rationalizing the ways we impose sentences, monetary sanctions, and bail payments can make our court system fairer, smarter, and more cost-effective. Finally, fixing cell block conditions and providing more skill and job training, mental health services and access to education for inmates can reduce barriers to reentry and decrease recidivism.

The Community

Early Childhood Education and Targeted Prevention Programs for Youth

Education interventions can prevent crime by improving future employment outcomes and reducing individuals' propensity to engage in risky behavior (see "Employment, Wage, and Education Policy and Crime Reduction" section). Economic research finds that investments in early childhood education can reduce crime and incarceration later in life, in part through improving subsequent educational attainment and reducing school dropout rates (CEA 2016; Currie 2001). Meanwhile, targeted education intervention programs for young adults can have large impacts on changing criminal behavior in the near-term and reducing recidivism (CEA 2015a).

Recognizing the benefits of early childhood education, the Administration has prioritized expanding access to high-quality preschool. Through the American Recovery and Reinvestment Act, President Obama supported $2.1 billion in Head Start and Early Head Start investments. In his 2013 State of the Union address, President Obama called upon Congress to expand access to high-quality preschool for every child in America. Since then, 37 States and D.C. have increased funding for their preschool programs by $1.5 billion. Through the Preschool Development Grants

(PDG) program, 18 States have received new Federal funding to expand the reach of their high-quality preschool programs in over 200 high-need communities.

The Administration has also invested in targeted education intervention programs for young adults. The President launched the My Brother's Keeper Initiative in 2014 to address persistent education and opportunity gaps among boys and young men of color and to ensure that all young people can reach their full potential, including an emphasis on reducing the risks of violent crime for young people. The President's 2017 Budget proposes $334.4 million for the Justice Department's Juvenile Justice Programs and includes evidence-based investments to prevent youth violence. The Budget also proposes $5.5 billion in new investments to connect more than 1 million young people to first jobs over the summer and year-round. In addition, in 2014, the President announced the designation of 5 Promise Zone communities, to partner with local communities and businesses to expand economic and educational opportunity and improve public safety.

Finally, the Administration has worked to promote safe and productive learning environments that keep children in school and reduce involvement with the criminal justice system. Once in public school, students may face harsh discipline policies that can obstruct learning and create a pipeline from schools to prisons. A study of over 1 million students in Texas found that 60 percent of students were suspended or expelled between the 7th and 12th grade, and Black students were 30 percent more likely to receive a discretionary disciplinary action (Council of State Governments 2011). Recognizing this problem, the Departments of Education (ED) and Justice (DOJ) established the Supportive School Discipline Initiative in 2011, which has issued guidance on best practices for public school districts and launched a Civil Rights database of disciplinary actions in over 7,000 districts across the country.

Community Policing and Policing Transparency

Economic research has consistently shown that police effectively reduce crime (see "Police and Crime Reduction" section). However, while the number of police officers per capita was relatively constant over the last two decades, the U.S. trails the international policing average by about a third (FBI UCR Data; Harrendorf, Heiskanen, and Malby 2010). This comparison suggests that increasing or altering investments in law enforcement and data-driven policing strategies, represent promising areas for reform.

There are also ways that law enforcement can improve their relationship with the communities that they serve, without compromising safety. A growing conversation about policing issues, including use of force and the role of race in police and community relations, has highlighted areas where law enforcement agencies may need to invest in training and change tactics. Experts in law enforcement and criminal justice advocates believe that community policing and enhanced police transparency are strategies that can improve safety and build trust (Police Executive Research Forum 2015; Goodman 2015).

In 2014, the President commissioned a Task Force on 21st Century Policing, as part of an effort to help communities and law enforcement strengthen trust and collaboration while continuing to reduce crime. This year, the Community Oriented Policing (COPS) at DOJ is coordinating with local communities and law enforcement to implement the recommendations from the Task Force. The White House established the Police Data Initiative to further these goals by working with over 30 police departments across the country to open data sets to the public and improve data collection systems. In September 2015, DOJ awarded $20 million in grants to 73 law enforcement and tribal agencies to purchase body-worn cameras, which research has found can reduce use-of-force incidents and citizens' complaints (Ariel, Farrar, and Sutherland 2015).The COPS office has also awarded over $1.5 billion in hiring grants to local police forces since 2009, providing funding support for over 9,000 officers.

Employment Restrictions: Record Expungement, "Ban-the-Box", and Occupational Licensing Exclusions

Having a criminal record or a prior history of incarceration can result in major barriers to securing a job (see "Collateral Consequences in the Labor Market" section). The American Bar Association National Inventory of Collateral Consequences of Conviction documents over 46,000 State and Federal laws restricting employment, occupational licenses, and business licenses for people with criminal records (American Bar Association 2016). As discussed above, policies that improve access to employment and sufficient wages for individuals with criminal records not only benefit individuals and their families, but also have the potential to decrease recidivism and increase the economic viability of communities.

The Administration is taking steps to reduce regulatory barriers to employment for people with criminal records while protecting public safety. The President has directed the Office of Personnel Management (OPM) to modify its rules to delay inquiries into criminal history until later in the Federal hiring process. He has also called on Congress to build on this announcement, following a growing number of States, cities, and private companies that have already decided to "ban the box" on job applications. In addition, as part of the Administration's ongoing work on occupational licensing, the White House is encouraging States to refrain from categorically excluding individuals with criminal records from occupational licenses, and instead to target criminal records that are recent and relevant, and pose a threat to public safety (CEA et al. 2015). The DOJ and Departments of Labor (DOL) have partnered to establish a National Clean Slate Clearinghouse to provide technical assistance to local legal aid programs, public defender offices, and reentry service providers to help with record-cleaning and expungement. In addition, DOJ and the Department of Housing and Urban Development (HUD) will provide $1.75 million to aid eligible public housing residents under the age of 25 to expunge or seal their records.

Access to Housing and Health Care

Individuals with limited resources may be denied public housing assistance for low-level offenses, such as prior alcohol and drug use. Further, incarcerated individuals also disproportionately suffer from chronic diseases, HIV, mental illness, and substance abuse, and have poor access to health care and may be excluded from important supportive programs after they are released (see "Collateral Consequences for Health, Financial Stability, Transportation, Housing, and Food Security" section; Wilper et al. 2009).

The Administration is implementing several measures to assist individuals with criminal records access housing and health care. HUD and the Bureau of Justice Assistance at DOJ have launched an $8.7 million demonstration grant to address homelessness and reduce recidivism among the justice-involved population. The Pay for Success (PFS) Permanent Supportive Housing Demonstration will test cost-effective ways to help persons cycling between the criminal justice and homeless service systems, while making new Permanent Supportive Housing available for the reentry population. In October 2015, DOJ announced $6 million in awards under the Second Chance Act to support reentry programming for adults with co-occurring substance abuse and mental disorders. In addition, the Centers for Medicare and Medicaid Services funded a Health Care Innovation Award in 2012 for a network that links patients with a chronic medical condition leaving prison to primary care in the community.

Criminal Justice System Databases and Reporting

Designing effective criminal justice system reform requires research and evaluation of policy approaches, which in turn necessitates accessible and comprehensive data on criminal justice system indicators. Currently, most national criminal justice data sets consist of voluntary reports by law enforcement or are derived from surveys of individuals or facilities. In many cases, data series are not formally or thoroughly audited due to resource constraints and may provide limited content or geographic coverage (NAJCD 2015).The nature of voluntary reporting without formal auditing may cause measurement error and can create challenges in analyzing data.

For example, the Uniform Crime Report (UCR) "Offenses Known and Crimes Cleared by Arrest" series, the most widely used data series for national and local crime trends, tracks total crime counts in only seven categories of reported crimes: murder and non-negligent manslaughter, rape, robbery, aggravated assault, burglary, larceny, and motor vehicle theft. These crime categories were originally chosen because of the relatively high likelihood of individuals reporting these crimes to the police, and these categories have been consistently collected since the establishment of the UCR in 1930. In an effort to build on the traditional UCR series and provide more detail for each reported crime at the incident level, UCR added the National Incident Based Reporting System (NIBRS) in 1987, but higher reporting burdens on law enforcement agencies has slowed the adoption of this system and limited its geographic coverage (FBI 2013). As part of a broader push to improve data transparency and accountability in the criminal justice system, the Administration is working with the Department of Justice and State and local governments to convert all law enforcement agency crime reporting to NIBRS from traditional UCR reporting and working to expand transparency around policing activity through the Police Data Initiative (FBI 2014; Police Foundation 2016).

Sentencing Reform

As discussed in detail in the Economic Framework section of this report, the total costs of incarceration in the United States exceed its benefits. However, the net efficiency of prison and jail varies by offender type, and sentencing reform is most constructive for low-risk offenders, for whom long sentences are especially inefficient (CCTF 2016).

The Administration has strongly supported sentencing reform, pursuing policies that reduce the prison population and apply sentences that are proportional to crimes committed. In 2010, President Obama signed the Fair Sentencing Act into law, which reduced the disparity in mandatory minimum sentences for crack cocaine and powder cocaine possession. In 2014, the independent United States Sentencing Commission (USSC) voted to amend Federal sentencing guidelines for certain drug crimes with support from the DOJ. This change in sentencing guidelines will prospectively reduce the Federal prison population by 6,500 prisoners over 5 years (USSC 2014). Since the beginning of the Administration, the President has commuted sentences for 248 Federal prisoners, most of whom were incarcerated for non-violent drug crimes. In 2010, the Bureau of Justice Assistance launched the Justice Reinvestment Initiative (JRI), which provides technical assistance to States and localities as they collect and analyze data on drivers of criminal justice populations—including sentencing practices—and identify and implement changes to reduce correctional spending and reinvest in strategies that decrease crime. Over the past year, criminal justice reform bills that focus on reducing mandatory minimums sentences for certain classes of offenders have been proposed in both the House and Senate and have been voted out of the House and Senate Judiciary Committee with strong bipartisan support and the Administration is working with Congress to support this legislative effort.

Fines, Fees, and Bail

Monetary sanctions and bail payments are typically not determined with an individual's ability to pay in mind, and so these payments disproportionately impact the poor (see "Collateral Consequences for Health, Financial Stability, Transportation, Housing, and Food Security" section). Criminal justice debts are often assigned to individuals unable to pay in full, making debt collection costly to the government and on net inefficient. Though fines and fees may be initially charged for minor offenses, the burden of these payments can increase for individuals that cannot pay them on time, with late fees, processing fees, interest, and even incarceration for failure to pay these debts. Likewise, because bail is typically assigned without consideration for an individual's resources, financial bail policies often result in detaining the poorest rather than the most dangerous offenders.

In March, DOJ announced new guidance and resources to assist state and local reform of fees and fines practices, and issued a "Dear Colleague Letter" to provide greater clarity to state and local courts regarding their legal obligations with respect to the enforcement of court fines and fees and a Resource Guide that assembles issue studies and other publications related to the assessment and enforcement of court fines and fees. DOJ also announced a $2.5 million competitive grant program to fund the development of strategies that promote appropriate justice system responses, including reducing unnecessary confinement, for individuals who are unable to pay fines and fees.

Given concerns about the growing use of financial bail, the 2011 National Symposium on Pretrial Justice outlined options for pretrial reform, with a focus on evidence-based policies like risk-assessment release models that use data on offense type and criminal history to determine non-financial pretrial release.

Drug Court Diversion Programs and Problem-Solving Courts

Problem-solving courts, including Drug Courts, Veterans Courts, and Mental Health Courts, are specialized courts that focus on particular offense types or offender populations. These courts offer alternative treatment and case management services in order to improve offender rehabilitation and reduce recidivism and vary in their eligibility requirements and rehabilitation approaches. Given a growing body of evaluation evidence of their success in reducing prison overcrowding and recidivism, problem-solving courts have rapidly expanded since the first drug court was established in 1989 (GAO 2005). Today, there are over 2,000 drug courts and over 1,000 other problem-solving courts operating across the country (Huddleston and Marlowe 2011).

Data from Florida show that counties that divert more defendants (or defer more prosecutions) prior to trial have higher rates of success, where success is defined as a prosecution or criminal sanction that is dropped when a defendant completes drug treatment or meets other requirements of the court (Figure 36). This relationship suggests that expertise and experience in offering diversion options improves defendant outcomes (Measures for Justice, Figure 36).[46]

---

[46] A deferred prosecution is an agreement between a defendant and the court that the defendant will not be prosecuted if he/she meets certain conditions (including but not limited to drug treatment offered through drug courts). Similarly, pretrial diversion requires individual defendants to fulfil certain requirements in order to avoid a court sanction that has already been assigned through court proceedings. Success in this context means that the defendant met the requirements of a deferral or diversion.

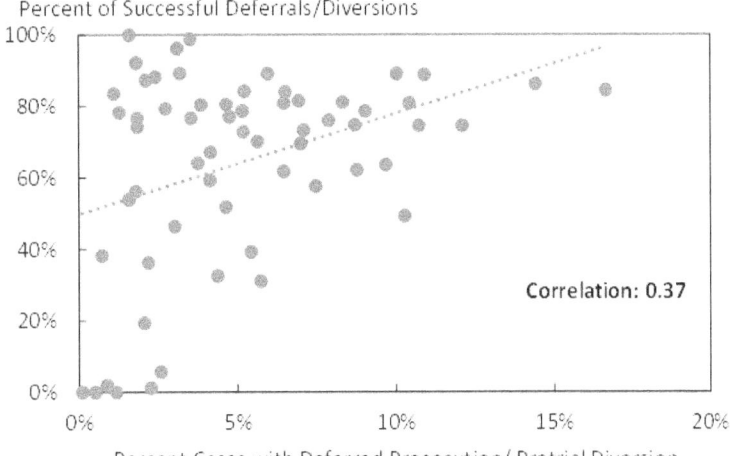

Figure 37:
Pretrial Diversion Success, Florida 2009-2013

Drug court diversion programs are designed to divert non-violent drug offenders from prison to drug treatment with rigorous accountability standards, and approach drug offenses as health issue rather than strictly a crime problem. The Bureau of Justice Assistance at DOJ has provided over $200 million in grants and technical assistance for local problem-solving courts throughout the Administration. DOJ's U.S. Attorneys' Offices participate in diversion and reentry courts in judicial districts across the country.

The Cell Block

Correctional Education, Rehabilitation Programs, and Job Training

Programs that support successful rehabilitation and provide opportunities for prisoners to build labor market skills are a critical to eliminating barriers to reentry and reducing recidivism. Participation rates in correctional education are low; available data shows that despite most prisons offering these programs, only about half of prison inmates participate, and while over 20 percent of inmates attend GED classes, less than 10 percent earn a high school degree (Harlow 2003).

Raising correctional education participation could lower re-offending rates and increase post-release employment and earnings (Hull et al. 2000; Chappell 2004); one study finds that participation in a prison GED program is associated with earnings gains of approximately 15 percent following release, though this effect is concentrated on non-Whites and declines over time (Tyler and Kling 2007). Tailored education and cognitive behavioral therapy interventions for juveniles in detention are promising areas for investment, with some programs reducing recidivism by 20 to 40 percent (Heller et al. 2015; Seroczynski et al. 2015).

The Administration has invested in rehabilitation programs in prisons and jails as part of a broader effort to give released prisoners a better chance at successfully starting over. In 2011, the Federal Interagency Reentry Council was established to identify and reduce barriers to reentry in employment, education, housing, health, and other key reentry areas. As part of this effort, DOL has awarded $10 million in grants to provide One Stop Career Center/American Jobs Centers services directly in local jails and $3 million to provide technology-based career training for incarcerated individuals. In July 2015, DOJ and ED announced the Second Chance Pell Pilot Program, which allows incarcerated Americans to receive Pell Grants for postsecondary education.

The Administration has also advocated for non-correctional education and job training programs for individuals who have already been released. In 2015, ED announced $8 million in Adult Reentry Education Grants, to support evidence-based programs that assist individuals after release. Likewise, DOL has awarded $27.5 million in Training to Work grants to provide workforce-related reentry programs for formerly incarcerated individuals. In a partnership with private sector stakeholders, the Center for Employment Opportunities Transitional Jobs Program has committed to expanding comprehensive employment services to people with recent criminal convictions, from 4,500 to 11,000 people served. Lastly, the President's TechHire initiative has worked with local communities and national employers to provide fast track technology training for individuals with criminal records.

Solitary Confinement

Research suggests that solitary confinement can lead to lasting psychological consequences and has been linked to a range of mental health conditions, including depression, anxiety, and withdrawal, along with the potential for violent behavior (Haney 2003). While estimates of the prevalence of solitary confinement vary, recent research finds that its use is widespread; in 2012, almost 20 percent of prison inmates and 18 percent of jail inmates reported spending time in restricted housing in the past 12 months or since coming to their current facility. Certain categories of prison inmates were especially likely to have reported spending time in restrictive housing during the past 12 months, including prisoners with less than a high school education and prisoners who had a history of mental health problems (Figure 38; Beck 2015).

Figure 38:
Incarcerated Individuals who spent time in Restricted Housing, 2011-2012

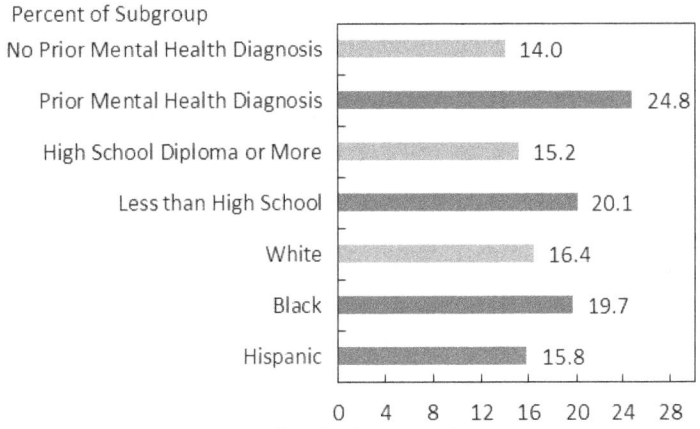

Note: Rates are weighted averages for Jail and Prison populations.
Source: Bureau of Justice Statistics, Beck (2015), "Use of Restrictive Housing in Prisons and Jails, 2011-12," CEA Calculations.

In July 2015, the President directed Attorney General Loretta E. Lynch and the DOJ to review the use of solitary confinement across U.S. prisons. Since then, DOJ has identified a set of common-sense principles that should guide the use of solitary confinement, including: housing inmates in the least restrictive settings necessary for safety reasons; ensuring that restrictions on an inmate's housing serve a specific penological purpose and are imposed for no longer than necessary; and ending the practice of placing juveniles in restrictive housing (DOJ 2015). This past January, the President adopted DOJ's recommendations to reform the use of solitary confinement in the Federal prison system, including banning solitary confinement for juvenile offenders and as a response to low-level infractions, expanding treatment for the mentally ill, and increasing the amount of time inmates in solitary can spend outside of their cells. These steps will affect some 10,000 federal prisoners held in solitary confinement, and will hopefully serve as a model for state and local corrections systems.

IV.   Conclusion

The evidence for criminal justice reform is mounting. Although crime rates are historically low, our criminal justice system incarcerates 2.2 million people, costs taxpayers hundreds of billions of dollars each year, and imposes substantial indirect consequences on justice system-involved individuals, their families, and communities. These consequences can include not only negative impacts on employment, but also health, debt, transportation, housing, and food security. They are disproportionately borne by Black and Hispanic men, poor individuals, and individuals with high rates of mental illness and substance abuse.

At the same time, economic research suggests that there are several policies that would make our criminal justice system more cost-effective and equitable. Research finds that investments in police and policies that improve labor market opportunity and educational attainment are more cost-effective than additional incarceration and can reduce the collateral consequences of convictions. Offering more correctional education and job training for inmates and the formerly incarcerated can reduce barriers to reentry and decrease recidivism. Reconsidering the ways we impose sentences, monetary sanctions, and bail payments can make our criminal justice system fairer and smarter.

The Obama Administration has taken a number of steps to make our criminal justice system more effective, efficient, and equitable. The Administration has invested in targeted prevention programs for youth and early childhood education to reduce crime both in the near-term and over the long-run. The Administration has promoted community policing and enhanced police transparency to improve community safety and build trust, and worked to change employment restrictions and expand access to health care and housing to reduce the collateral consequences of convictions. In addition, the Administration has implemented new policies to provide skill and job training, mental health services and access to education for inmates to reduce barriers to reentry and decrease recidivism.

Over the coming year, the Administration will continue to pursue reform within the Executive Branch and work with Congress to pass meaningful criminal justice reform legislation.

References

Aizer, Anna and Joseph J. Doyle, Jr. 2013. "Juvenile Incarceration, Human Capital and Future Crime: Evidence From Randomly-Assigned Judges." *National Bureau of Economic Research*. Working Paper 19102.

Albonetti, Celesta A. 2016. "Mandatory minimum penalties." In *Advancing Criminology and Criminal Justice Policy*, edited by Thomas G. Bloomberg, Julie Mestre Brancale, Kevin M. Beaver, and William D. Bales. London: Routledge.

American Bar Association. 2016. "National Inventory of Collateral Consequences of Conviction." *American Bar Association*. <http://www.abacollateralconsequences.org/search/>.

Anderson, David. 1999. "The Aggregate Burden of Crime." *Journal of Law and Economics* 42(2):611-642.

Anderson, D. Mark. 2014. "In School and Out of Trouble? The Minimum Dropout Age and Juvenile Crime." *The Review of Economics and Statistics* 96(2): 318-331.

Antonovics, Kate and Brian G. Knight. 2009. "A New Look at Racial Profiling: Evidence From the Boston Police Department." *The Review of Economics and Statistics* 91(1): 163-177.

Anwar, Shamena, Patrick Bayer, and Randi Hjalmarsson. 2012. "The Impact of Jury Race in Criminal Trials." *The Quarterly Journal of Economics* (2012) 127: 1017–1055.

Anwar, Shamena and Hanming Fang. 2006. "An Alternative Test of Racial Prejudice in Motor Vehicle Searches: Theory and Evidence." *The American Economic Review* 96 (1): 127-151.

Ariel, Barak, William A. Farrar, and Alex Sutherland. 2015. "The Effect of Policy Body-Worn Cameras on Use of Force and Citizens' Complaints Against the Policy: A Randomized Controlled Trial." *Journal of Quantitative Criminology* 31: 509–535.

Ashenfelter, Orley. 2006. "Measuring the Value of a Statistical Life: Problems and Prospects." *The Economic Journal* 116(510): C10-C23.

Bannon, Alicia, Mitali Nagrecha, and Rebekah Diller. 2010. "Criminal Justice Debt: A Barrier to Reentry." The Brennan Center for Justice.

Bar-Ilan, Avner and Bruce Sacerdote. 2004. "The Response of Criminals and Noncriminals to Fines." *Journal of Law and Economics* 47(1): 1-17.

Baradaran, Shima and Frank L. McIntyre. 2012. "Predicting Violence." *Texas Law Review* 90 (1): 497-570.

Bayer, Patrick, Randi Hjalmarsson, and David Pozen. 2009. "Building Criminal Capital Behind Bars: Peer Effects in Juvenile Corrections." *The Quarterly Journal of Economics* 124 (1): 105-147.

Beck, Allen J. 2015. "Use of Restrictive Housing in U.S. Prisons and Jails, 2011-12." U.S. Department of Justice, Bureau of Justice Statistics.

Beck, Allen J., Marcus Berzofsky, Rachel Caspar, and Christopher Krebs. 2013. "Sexual Victimization in Prisons and Jails Reported by Inmates, 2011-12." *Bureau of Justice Statistics, U.S. Department of Justice.*

Becker, Gary. 1968. "Crime and Punishment: An Economic Approach." *Journal of Political Economy* 76 (2): 169-217.

Beckett, Katherine and Alexes Harris. 2011. "On cash and conviction: Monetary sanctions as misguided policy." *Criminology & Public Policy* 10(3): 509-537.

Beckett, Katherine, Alexes Harris, and Heather Evans. 2008. "The Assessment and Consequences of Legal Financial Obligations in Washington State." Washington State Minority and Justice Commission.

Beitsch, Rebecca. 2015. "States Rethink Restrictions on Food Stamps, Welfare for Drug Felons." The Pew Charitable Trusts. < http://www.pewtrusts.org/en/research-and-analysis/blogs/stateline/2015/07/30/states-rethink-restrictions-on-food-stamps-welfare-for-drug-felons>.

Belfield, Clive R., Milagros Nores, Steve Barnett, and Lawrence Schweinhart. 2006. "The High/Scope Perry Preschool Program: Cost-Benefit Analysis Using Data from the Age-40 Followup." The Journal of Human Resources 41(1): 162-190.

Bell, Brian, Laura Jaitman, and Stephen Machin. 2013. "Crime Deterrence: Evidence From the London 2011 Riots" Working Paper.

Bernburg, Jön Gunnar and Marvin D. Krohn. 2003. "Labeling, Life Chances, and Adult Crime: The Direct and Indirect Effects of Official Intervention in Adolescence on Crime in Early Adulthood." Criminology 41(4): 1287-1318.

Blumstein, Alfred and Kiminori Nakamura. 2009. "Redemption in the Presence of Widespread Criminal Background." Criminology 47(2): 327-359.

Bonczar, Thomas P. 2003. "Prevalence of Imprisonment in the U.S. Population, 1974-2001." Bureau of Justice Statistics, U.S Department of Justice.

Boylan, Richard T. and Naci Mocan. 2013. "Intended and Unintended Consequences of Prison Reform." The Journal of Law and Economics 30(3): 558-586.

Braga, Anthony, Andrew Papachristos and David Hureau. 2014. "The Effects of Hot Spots Policing on Crime: An Updated Systematic Review and Meta-Analysis." Justice Quarterly 31(4): 633-663.

Bureau of Labor Statistics. 2016. "Occupational Employment and Wages, May 2015: Police and Sheriff's Patrol Officers". United States Department of Labor.

Bureau of Justice Statistics. 1980-2014. "Prisoners" Series. U.S. Department of Justice.

Bureau of Justice Statistics. 1980-2014. "Jail Inmates at Midyear" Series. U.S. Department of Justice.

Bureau of Justice Statistics. 1980-2012. "Justice Expenditures and Employment Extracts" Series. United States Department of Justice. <http://www.bjs.gov/index.cfm?ty=dcdetail&iid=286>.

Bureau of Justice Statistics. 1990-2009. "Felony Defendants in Large Urban Counties" Series. U.S. Department of Justice.

Bureau of Justice Statistics. 2016. "Data Collection: National Judicial Reporting Program (NJRP) 1986-2006." United States Department of Justice. <http://www.bjs.gov/index.cfm?ty=dcdetail&iid=241>.

Bureau of Justice Statistics. 2012. "Survey of State Criminal History Information Systems." United States Department of Justice.

Bureau of Justice Statistics. 2016. "Arrest Data Analysis Tool." United States Department of Justice. <http://www.bjs.gov/index.cfm?ty=datool&surl=/arrests/index.cfm>.

Bushway, Shawn D., Philip J. Cook, and Matthew Phillips. 2010. "The net effect of the business cycle on crime and violence." Working Paper.

Bushway, Shawn D. and Emily G. Owens. 2013. "Framing Punishment: Incarceration, Recommended Sentences, and Recidivism." *Journal of Law & Economics* 56(2): 301-331.

Caetano, Gregorio and Vikram Maheshri. 2013. "Do 'Broken Windows' Matter? Identifying Dynamic Spillovers in Criminal Behavior." Working Paper.

Carson, E. Ann. 2015. "Prisoners in 2014." *Bureau of Justice Statistics, U.S. Department of Justice.*

Center for Constitutional Rights. 2012. "Stop and Frisk – The Human Impact." *The Center for Constitutional Rights.*

Chalfin, Aaron and Justin McCrary. 2013. "The Effect of Police on Crime: New Evidence from U.S. Cities, 1960-2010." The National Bureau of Economic Research. Working Paper 18815.

Chalfin, Aaron and Justin McCrary. 2014. "Criminal Deterrence: A Review of the Literature." Working Paper.

Chandra, Amitabh. 2000. "Labor-Market Dropouts and the Racial Wage Gap: 1940-1990." *The American Economic Review* 90 (2): 333-338.

Chappell, Cathryn A. 2004. "Post-Secondary Correctional Education and Recidivism: A Meta-Analysis of Research Conducted 1990-1999." *The Journal of Correctional Education* 55(2): 148-169.

Charles Colson Task Force on Federal Corrections. 2016. "Transforming Prisons, Restoring Lives: Final Recommendations of the Charles Colson Task Force on Federal Corrections." Urban Institute.

Chen, M. Keith and Jesse M. Shapiro. 2007. "Do Harsher Prison Conditions Reduce Recidivism? A Discontinuity-based Approach." *American Law and Economics Review* 9(1): 1-29.

Cohen, Jacqueline and Jens Ludwig. 2003. "Policing Crime Guns." In *Evaluating Gun Policy: Effects on Crime and Violence,* Jens Ludwig and Philip J. Cook eds. *The Brookings Institution.*

Cohen, Mark A. 1988. "Pain, Suffering, and Jury Awards: A Study of the Cost of Crime to Victims." *Law & Society Review* 22(3): 537-556.

Cohen, Mark, Roland Rust, Sara Steen and Simon Tidd. 2004. "Willingness-to-Pay for Crime Control Programs." *Criminology* 42(1): 89-109.

Conduct Problems Prevention Research Group. 2007. "Fast Track Randomized Controlled Trial to Prevent Externalizing Psychiatric Disorders: Findings From Grades 3 to 9." *Journal of the American Academy of Child and Adolescent Psychiatry* 46(10): 1250-1262.

Council of Economic Advisers (CEA). 2015a. "Economic Costs of Youth Disadvantage and High-Return Opportunities for Change."

CEA. 2015b. "Fines, Fees and Bail: Payments in the Criminal Justice System that Disproportionately Impact the Poor."

CEA, Department of the Treasury Office of Economic Policy, and Department of Labor. 2015. "Occupational Licensing: A Framework for Policymakers" <https://www.whitehouse.gov/sites/default/files/docs/licensing_report_final_nonembargo.pdf>.

CEA. 2016. *Economic Report of the President*. February.

Cullen, Julie Berry, Brian A. Jacob, and Steven Levitt. 2006. "The Effect of School Choice on Participants: Evidence from Randomized Lotteries." *Econometrica* 74(5): 1191-1230.

Currie, Janet. 2001. "Early Childhood Education Programs." *Journal of Economic Perspectives* 15 (2): 213-238.

Curtis, Marah A., Sarah Garlington, and Lisa S. Schottenfeld. 2013. "Alcohol, Drug, and Criminal History Restrictions in Public Housing." *Cityscape: A Journal of Policy Development and Research* 15(3): 37-52.

Dansky, Kara. 2016. "Local Democratic Oversight of Police Militarization." *Harvard Law Review* 10: 59-75.

DeAngelo, Gregory and Benjamin Hansen. 2014. "Life and Death in the Fast Lane: Police Enforcement and Traffic Fatalities." *American Economic Journal: Economic Policy* 6(2): 231-257.

Deming, David. 2009a. "Better Schools, Less Crime?" Working Paper.

Devers, Lindsey. 2011. "Plea and Charge Bargaining: Research Summary." *Bureau of Justice Assistance, U.S. Department of Justice.*

Diller, Rebekah. 2010. "The Hidden Costs of Florida's Criminal Justice Fees." The Brennan Center for Justice.

Diller, Rebekah, Judith Greene, and Michelle Jacobs. 2009. "Maryland's Parole Supervision Fee: A Barrier to Reentry." *The Brennan Center for Justice.*

Donohue, John J. and Peter Siegelman. 1998. "Allocating Resources Among Prisons and Social Programs In The Battle Against Crime." *The Journal of Legal Studies* 27(1):1-43.

Donohue, John. 2009. "Assessing the Relative Benefits of Incarceration: The Overall Change Over the Previous Decades and the Benefits on the Margin." In *Do Prisons Make Us Safer? The Benefits and Costs of the Prison Boom,* Raphael, Stephen and Michael Stoll, eds. Russell Sage Foundation, New York, NY.

Doyle, Joanne M., Ehsan Ahmed, and Robert N. Horn. 1999. "The Effects of Labor Markets and Income Inequality on Crime: Evidence from Panel Data." *Southern Economic Journal* 65(4): 717-738.

Drago, Francesco, Roberto Galbiati, and Pietro Vertova. 2009. "The Deterrent Effects of Prison: Evidence from a Natural Experiment." *The Journal of Political Economy* 117(2): 257-80.

Durlauf, Steven N. and Daniel S. Nagin. "The Deterrent Effect of Imprisonment." In *Controlling Crime: Strategies and Tradeoff,* edited by Philip J. Cook, Jens Ludwig, and Justin McCrary, 43-94. Chicago: University of Chicago Press, 2011.

Durose, Matthew R, Alexia D. Cooper, and Howard N. Snyder. 2014. "Recidivism of Prisoners Released in 30 States in 2005: Patterns from 2005 to 2010." *Office of Justice Programs, U.S. Department of Justice.*

Eberhardt, Jennifer L., Phillip Atiba Goff, Valerie J. Purdie, and Paul G. Davies. 2004. "Seeing Black: Race, Crime, and Visual Processing." *Journal of Personality and Social Psychology* 87(6): 876-893.

Evans, William and Emily Owens. 2007. "COPS and crime." *Journal of Public Economics* 91: 181-201.

Evans, William N., Craig Garthwaite, and Timothy J. Moore. 2012. "The White/Black Educational Gap, Stalled Progress, and the Long Term Consequences of the Emergence of Crack Cocaine Markets." Working Paper 18437. *National Bureau of Economic Research.*

Fabelo, Tony, Michael D. Thompson, Martha Plotkin, Dottie Carmicheal, Miner P. Marchbanks III, and Eric A. Booth. 2011. "Breaking Schools' Rules: A Statewide Study of How School Discipline Relates to Students' Success and Juvenile Justice Involvement." The Council of

State Governments Justice Center and the Public Policy Research Institute, Texas A&M University.

Federal Bureau of Investigation. 1980-2014. "Crime in the United States – Uniform Crime Reports." *U.S. Department of Justice*.

Federal Bureau of Investigation. 2013. "National Incident Based Reporting System (NIBRS) User Manual." *FBI Uniform Crime Reports*. < https://www.fbi.gov/about-us/cjis/ucr/nibrs/nibrs-user-manual>.

Federal Bureau of Investigation. 2014. "Message from the Director." *FBI Uniform Crime Reports*. <https://www.fbi.gov/about-us/cjis/ucr/crime-in-the-u.s/2014/crime-in-the-u.s.-2014/resource-pages/message-from-director>.

Federal Bureau of Investigation. 1994-2014. "Crime in the United States by Volume and Rate per 100,000 Inhabitants, 1994-2014." *FBI Uniform Crime Reports*. < https://www.fbi.gov/about-us/cjis/ucr/crime-in-the-u.s/2013/crime-in-the-u.s.2013/tables/1tabledatadecoverviewpdf/table_1_crime_in_the_united_states_by_volume_and_rate_per_100000_inhabitants_1994-2013.xls>.

FindLaw. 2016. "What Conduct Could Lead to Driver's License Revocation?" *Thomson Reuters*. <http://traffic.findlaw.com/drivers-license-vehicle-info/what-conduct-could-lead-to-drivers-license-revocation.html/>.

Fryer, Roland G., Paul S. Heaton, Steven D. Levitt, and Kevin M. Murphy. 2013. "Measuring Crack Cocaine and Its Impact." *Economic Inquiry* 51(3): 1651-1681.

Gelber, Alexander, Adam Isen, Judd B. Kessler. "The Effects of Youth Employment: Evidence from New York City Lotteries." Working Paper.

Geller, Amanda, Irwin Garfinkel, and Bruce Western. 2006. "The Effects of Incarceration on Employment and Wages: An Analysis of the Fragile Families Survey." Center for Research on Child Wellbeing. Working Paper 2006-01-FF.

Gill, Charlotte, David Weisburd, and Cody Telep. "Community Policing." *Advancing Criminology and Criminal Justice Policy*.

Glaze, Lauren E., and Laura M. Maruschak. 2008. "Parents in Prison and Their Minor Children." *Bureau of Justice Statistics Special Report*.

Goodman, David J. 2015. "In New York, Testing Grounds for Community Policing." *The New York Times*. < http://www.nytimes.com/2015/08/24/nyregion/for-new-york-police-a-radical-change-for-queens-residents-a-step.html?_r=0>.

Gould, Eric D., Bruce A. Weinberg, and David B. Mustard. 2002. "Crime Rates and Local Labor Market Opportunities in the United States: 1979-1997." *The Review of Economics and Statistics* 84(1): 45-61.

Green, Donald P. and Daniel Winik. 2010. "Using Random Judge Assignments to Estimate the Effects of Incarceration and Probation on Recidivism Among Drug Offenders." *Criminology* 48(2): 357-387.

Grogger, Jeff. 1992. "Persistent Youth Joblessness, and Black/White Employment Differentials." *The Review of Economics and Statistics* 74(1): 100-106.

Grogger, Jeffrey. 1995. "The Effect of Arrests on the Employment and Earnings of Young Men." *The Quarterly Journal of Economics* 110(1): 51-71.

Grogger, Jeff. 1998. "Market Wages and Youth Crime." *Journal of Labor Economics* 16(4): 756-791.

Hall, Joshua C., Kaitlyn Harger, and Dean Stansel. 2015. "Economic Freedom and Recidivism: Evidence from US States." *International Advances in Economic Research* 21 (1): 155-165.

Haney, Craig. 2003. "Mental Health Issues in Long-Term Solitary and 'Supermax' Confinement." *Crime & Delinquency* 49(1): 124-156.

Harcourt, Bernard and Jens Ludwig. 2007. "Reefer Madness: Broken Windows Policing and Misdemeanor Marijuana Arrests in New York City, 1989-2000." *Criminology* 6(1): 165-181.

Harding, David J., Jeffrey D. Morenoff, and Claire W. Herbert. 2013. "Home is Hard to Find: Neighborhoods, Institutions, and the Residential Trajectories of Returning Prisoners." *Annals of the American Academy of Political and Social Science* 647: 214-236.

Harlow, Caroline Wolf. 2003. "Education and Correctional Populations." *Bureau of Justice Statistics.* Special Report.

Harrendorf, S., M. Heiskanen, and S. Malby. 2010. "International Statistics on Crime and Justice." *United Nations Office on Drugs and Crime.*

Harris, Benjamin and Melissa Kearney. April 28, 2014. "The Unequal Burden of Crime and Incarceration on America's Poor." *The Brookings Institution,* Washington, D.C. <http://www.brookings.edu/blogs/up-front/posts/2014/04/28-unequal-burden-crime-americas-poor-kearneym-harrisb>.

Hartney, Christopher, and Linh Vuong. 2009. "Created Equal: Racial and Ethnic Disparities in the US Criminal Justice System." *National Council on Crime and Delinquency.*

Hawken, Angela, and Mark Kleiman. 2009. "Managing Drug Involved Probationers with Swift and Certain Sanctions: Evaluating Hawaii's HOPE." U.S. Department of Justice.

Heckman, James J., Seong Hyeok Moon, Rodrigo Pinto, Peter A. Savelyev, Adam Yavitz. 2010. "The rate of return to the HighScope Perry Preschool Program." *Journal of Public Economics* 94(1): 114-128.

Helland, Eric, and Alexander Tabarrok. 2007. "Does Three Strikes Deter? A Nonparametric Estimation." *The Journal of Human Resources* 42(2): 309-330.

Heller, Sara B. 2014. "Summer Jobs Reduce Violence among Disadvantaged Youth." Working Paper.

Heller, Sara B., Anuj K. Shah, Jonathan Guryan, Jens Ludwig, Sendhil Mullainathan, Harold A. Pollack. 2015. "Thinking, Fast and Slow? Some Field Experiments to Reduce Crime and Dropout in Chicago." Working Paper 21178. *National Bureau of Economic Research.*

Henrichson, Christian and Ruth Delaney. 2012. "The Price of Prisons: What Incarceration Costs Taxpayers." *Vera Institute of Justice.*

Herberman, Erinn and Tracey Kyckelhahn. 2015. "State Government Indigent Defense Expenditures, FY 2008-2012 – Updated. *Bureau of Justice Statistics Special Report.*

Hjalmarsson, Randi. 2009a. "Juvenile Jails: A Path to the Straight and Narrow or to Hardened Criminality?" *Journal of Law and Economics* 52(4): 779-809.

Hjalmarsson, Randi. 2009b. "Crime and Expected Punishment: Changes in Perceptions at the Age of Criminal Majority." *American Law and Economics Review* 11(1): 209-248.

Hjalmarsson, Randi and Matthew J. Lindquist. 2012. "Like Godfather, Like Son: Exploring the Intergenerational Nature of Crime." *The Journal of Human Resources* 47(2): 550-582.

Holzer, Harry J., Paul Offner, and Elaine Sorenson. 2005. "Declining Employment Among Young Black Less-Educated Men: The Role of Incarceration and Child Support." *Journal of Policy Analysis and Management* 24(2): 329-350.

Holzer, Harry J., Steven Raphael, and Michael A. Stoll. 2006. "Perceived Criminality, Criminal Background Checks, and the Racial Hiring Practices of Employers." *Journal of Law and Economics* 49(2): 451-480.

Huddleston, West and Douglas B. Marlowe. 2011. "Painting the Current Picture: A National Report on Drug Courts and Other Problem-Solving Court Programs in the United States." *Office of National Drug Control Policy*, *Bureau of Justice Assistance*, and the *National Drug Court Institute*.

Hull, Kim A., Stewart Forrester, James Brown, David Jobe, Charles McCullen. 2000. "Analysis of Recidivism Rates for Participants of the Academic/Vocational/Transition Education Programs Offered by the Virginia Department of Correctional Education." *Journal of Correctional Education* 51(2): 256-61.

Hunt, Kim Steven, and Robert Dumville. 2016. "Recidivism Among Federal Offenders: A Comprehensive Overview." United States Sentencing Commission.

Ihlanfeldt, Keith R. 2007. "Neighborhood Drug Crime and Young Males' Job Accessibility." *The Review of Economics and Statistics* 89(1): 151-164.

Iyengar, Radha. 2008. "I'd Rather Be Hanged for a Sheep than a Lamb: The Unintended Consequences of 'Three-Strikes' Laws." Working paper 13784. *National Bureau of Economic Research*.

Jacob, Brian A., and Lars Lefgren. 2003. "Are Idle Hands the Devil's Workshop? Incapacitation, Concentration, and Juvenile Crime." *The American Economic Review* 93(5): 1560-1577.

James, Doris J. and Lauren E. Glaze. 2006. "Mental Health Problems of Prison and Jail Inmates." *Bureau of Justice Statistics Special Report*.

Johnson, Rucker. 2009. "Ever-Increasing Levels of Parental Incarceration and the Consequences for Children." *Do Prisons Make Us Safer?: The Benefits and Costs of the Prison Boom*. Raphael, Steven and Michael Stoll, Eds. New York: Russell Sage Foundation. 177-206.

Johnson, Rucker, and Steven Raphael. 2012. "How Much Crime Reduction does the Marginal Prisoner Buy?" *Journal of Law and Economics* 55(2): 275-310.

Justice Policy Institute. 2014. "Sticker Shock: Calculating the Full Price Tag for Youth Incarceration." *Justice Policy Institute*.

Juvenile Justice Initiative. 2016. "Raise the Age." *Juvenile Justice Initiative*. <http://jjustice.org/resources/raise-the-age/>.

Kang, Jay Caspian. 2015. "Our Demand is Simple: Stop Killing Us." *The New York Times*. <http://www.nytimes.com/2015/05/10/magazine/our-demand-is-simple-stop-killing-us.html>.

Kessler, Daniel, and Steven D. Levitt. 1999. "Using Sentence Enhancements to Distinguish Between Deterrence and Incapacitation." *Journal of Law and Economics* 42(1): 343-363.

Kindy, Kimberly, Marc Fisher, and Julie Tate. 2015 "A Year of Reckoning: Police Fatally Shoot Nearly 1,000." *The Washington Post*.

Klick, Jonathan and Alexander Tabarrok. 2005. "Using Terror Alert Levels to Estimate the Effect of Police on Crime." *Journal of Law and Economics* 48(1): 267-279.

Kling, Jeffrey R. 2006. "Incarceration Length, Employment, and Earnings." *Princeton University – Industrial Relations Section*. Working Paper 494.

Kovandzic, Tomislav V. 2001. "The Impact of Florida's Habitual Offender Law on Crime." *Criminology* 39(1): 179-204.

Kurlychek, Megan C., Robert Brame, and Shawn. D. Bushway. 2007. "Enduring Risk? Old Criminal Records and Predictions of Future Criminal Involvement." *Crime & Delinquency* 53(1): 64-83.

Kuziemko, Ilyana. 2013. "How Should Inmates Be Released From Prison? An Assessment of Parole Versus Fixed-Sentence Regimes." *The Quarterly Journal of Economics* (2013): 371–424.

Kuziemko, Ilyana and Steven D. Levitt. 2004. "An Empirical Analysis of Imprisoning Drug Offenders." *Journal of Public Economics* 88(9-10, August): 2043-2066.

Landersø, Rasmus. 2015. "Does Incarceration Length Affect Labor Market Outcomes?" *Journal of Law and Economics* 58(1): 205-234.

Langton, Lynn and Donald Farole. 2010. "State Public Defender Programs, 2007." *Bureau of Justice Statistics Special Report.*

Langton, Lynnand and Matthew Durose. 2013. "Police Behavior during Traffic and Street Stops, 2011." Bureau of Justice Statistics Special Report.

Lawrence, Alison. 2008. "Probation and Parole Violations: State Responses." *National Conference of State Legislatures.*

Lee, David S, and Justin McCrary. 2005. "Crime, Punishment, and Myopia." Working Paper 11491, *National Bureau of Economic Research.*

Lee, David S, and Justin McCrary. 2009. "The Deterrence Effect of Prison: Dynamic Theory and Evidence." Working Paper 1168, *Princeton University, Department of Economics.*

Levitt, Steven. 1996. "The Effect of Prison Population Size on Crime Rates: Evidence From Prison Overcrowding Litigation." *The Quarterly Journal of Economics.* 111(2): 319-351.

Levitt, Steven. 1997. "Using Electoral Cycles in Police Hiring to Estimate the Effect of Police on Crime." *The American Economic Review* 87(3): 270-290.

Levitt, Steven. 1999. "The Limited Role of Changing Age Structure in Explaining Aggregate Crime Rates." *Criminology* 37(3): 581-598.

Levitt, Steven. 2002. "Using Electoral Cycles in Police Hiring to Estimate the Effects of Police on Crime: Reply." *The American Economic Review* 92(4): 1244-1250.

Liedka, Raymond V., Anne Morrison Piehl, and Bert Useem. 2006. "The Crime-Control Effect of Incarceration: Does Scale Matter?" *Criminology and Public Policy* 5(2): 245-276.

Lin, Ming-Jen. 2009. "More police, less crime: Evidence from US state data." *International Review of Law and Economics* 29: 73-80.

Listenbee, Robert L. et al. 2012. "Report of the Attorney General's National Task Force on Children Exposed to Violence." U.S. Department of Justice.

Lochner, Lance. 2004. "Education, Work, and Crime: A Human Capital Approach." *International Economic Review* 45(3): 811-843.

Lochner, Lance and Enrico Moretti. 2004. "The Effect of Education on Crime: Evidence from Prison Inmates, Arrests, and Self-Reports." *The American Economic Review* 94(1): 155-189.

Lofstrom, Magnus, and Steven Raphael. 2013. "Public Safety Realignment and Crime Rates in California." Public Policy Institute of California.

Lovell, David, L. Clark Johnson, and Kevin C. Cain. 2007. "Recidivism of Supermax Prisoners in Washington State." *Crime and Delinquency* 53(1): 633-656.

Luallen, Jeremy. 2006. "School's out…forever: A study of juvenile crime, at-risk youths and teacher strikes." *Journal of Urban Economics* 59(2006): 75-103.

Markowitz, Sara. 2000. "An Economic Analysis of Alcohol, Drugs, and Violent Crime in the National Crime Victimization Survey." National Bureau of Economic Research. Working Paper 7982.

Massoglia, Michael. 2008. "Incarceration, Health, and Racial Disparities in Health." *Law and Society Review*, 42: 275-306.

Massoglia, Michael, Brianna Remster, and Ryan D. King. 2011. "Stigma or Separation? Understanding the Incarceration-Divorce Relationship." *Social Forces* 90(1): 133-155.

Matsueda, Ross L. 1992. "Reflected Appraisals, Parental Labeling, and Delinquency: Specifying a Symbolic Interactionist Theory." *American Journal of Sociology* 97(6): 1577-1611.

McCollister, Kathryn, Michael French and Hai Fang. 2010. "The Cost of Crime to Society: New Crime-Specific Estimates for Policy and Program Evaluation." *Drug and Alcohol Dependence* 108(1-2): 98-109.

McCrary, Justin. 2002. "Using Electoral Cycles in Police Hiring to Estimate the Effect of Police on Crime: Comment." *The American Economic Review* 92(4): 1236-1243.

Mears, Daniel P., and William D. Bales. 2009. "Supermax Incarceration and Recidivism." *Criminology* 47 (4): 1131-1166.

Measures for Justice. Florida data. 2016. Rochester, NY.

Minton, Todd D. and Zhen Zheng. 2015. "Jail Inmates at Midyear 2014." *Bureau of Justice Statistics*.

Miller, Ted, Mark Cohen and Brian Wiersema. 1996. "Victim Costs and Consequences: A New Look." National Institute of Justice Research Report, *National Institute of Justice*.

Mitchell, Michael and Michael Leachman. 2014. "Changing Priorities: State Criminal Justice Reforms and Investments in Education." *Center on Budget and Policy Priorities*.

Mueller-Smith, Michael. 2015. "The Criminal and Labor Market Impacts of Incarceration." Working Paper.

Murphey, David and P. Mae Cooper. 2015. "Parents Behind Bars: What Happens to Their Children?" Child Trends.

Murray, Joseph and David P. Farrington. 2008. "The Effects of Parental Imprisonment on Children." *Crime and Justice* 37(1): 133-206.

Nagin, Daniel S. and Joel Waldfogel. 1998. "The Effect of Conviction on Income Through the Life Cycle." *International Review of Law and Economics* 18(1): 25-40.

Nagin, Daniel S., Robert M. Solow, and Cynthia Lum. 2015. "Deterrence, Criminal Opportunities and Police." *Criminology* 53(1): 74-100.

National Archive of Criminal Justice Data (NACJD). "Codebook: Uniform Crime Reporting Program Data: Offenses Known and Clearances by Arrest, 2013." Accessed 8/2015. <http://www.icpsr.umich.edu/icpsrweb/NACJD/studies/36122>.

National Symposium on Pretrial Justice. 2011. "Summary Report of Proceedings." *A Publication of the Pretrial Justice Institute.*

Neal, Derek and Armin Rick. 2014. "The Prison Boom and the Lack of Black Progress after Smith and Welch." Working Paper 20283. *National Bureau of Economic Research.*

Neal, Melissa. 2012. "Bail Fail: Why the U.S. Should End the Practice of Using Money for Bail." Justice Policy Institute.

Office of Juvenile Justice and Delinquency Prevention. 2015. "Easy Acces to the Census of Juveniles in Residential Placement: 1997-2013." *Office of Justice Programs, U.S. Department of Justice.* < http://www.ojjdp.gov/ojstatbb/ezacjrp/>.

Oreopoulos, Philip and Kjell G. Salvanes. 2011. "Priceless: The Nonpecuniary Benefits of Schooling." *The Journal of Economic Perspectives* 25(1): 159-184.

Owens, Emily G. 2009. "More Time, Less Crime?: Estimating the Incapacitative Effect of Sentence Enhancements." *Journal of Law & Economics* 52(3): 551-579.

Owens, Emily G. 2011. "COPS and Cuffs." *Lessons From the Economics of Crime: What Works in Reducing Offending?.*

Pager, Devah. 2003. "The Mark of a Criminal Record." *American Journal of Sociology* 108(5): 937-975.

Pager, Devah, Bruce Western, and Naomi Sugie. 2009. "Sequencing Disadvantage: Barriers to Employment Facing Young Black and White Men with Criminal Records." *The Annals of the Academy of Political and Social Science* 623(1): 195–213.

The Pew Charitable Trusts. 2010. "Collateral Costs: Incarceration's Effect on Economic Mobility." Washington, D.C.: *The Pew Charitable Trusts.*

The Pew Charitable Trusts. 2015. "Prison Time Surges for Federal Inmates." Washington, DC: *The Pew Charitable Trusts.*

Phillips, Mary T. 2012. "A Decade of Bail Research in New York City." New York City Criminal Justice Agency, Inc.

Piehl, Anne Morrison and Geoffrey Williams. 2011. "Institutional Requirements for Effective Imposition of Fines." In *Controlling Crime: Strategies and Tradeoffs*, edited by Philip J. Cook, Jens Ludwig, and Justin McCrary, 95-121. Chicago: University of Chicago Press.

Planty, Michael, Lynn Langton, Christopher Krebs, Marcus Berzofsky, Hope Smiley-McDonald. 2013. "Female Victims of Sexual Violence, 1994-2010." Bureau of Justice Statistics.

Police Executive Research Forum. 2015. *Constitutional Policing as a Cornerstone of Community Policing: A Report by the Policy Executive Research Forum.* Washington, DC: Office of Community Oriented Policing Services.

Police Foundation. 2016. Public Safety Open Data Portal. <http://publicsafetydataportal.org/participating-agencies/>.

Rakoff, Jed S. "Why Innocent People Plead Guilty." *The New York Review of Books.* 20 November 2014. < http://www.nybooks.com/articles/2014/11/20/why-innocent-people-plead-guilty/>.

Raphael, Steven. 2006a. "Early Incarceration Spells and the Transition to Adulthood." *University of California, Berkeley*. Working Paper.

Raphael, Steven. 2011. "Improving Employment Prospects for Former Prison Inmates: Challenges and Policy." In *Controlling Crime: Strategies and Tradeoffs*, edited by Philip J. Cook, Jens Ludwig, and Justin McCrary, 521-565. Chicago: University of Chicago Press.

Raphael, Steven and Michael A. Stoll. 2013a. "Assessing the Contribution of the Deinstitutionalization of the Mentally Ill to Growth in the U.S. Incarceration Rate." *Journal of Legal Studies* 42: 187-222.

Raphael, Steven and Michael A. Stoll. 2013b. "Why Are So Many Americans in Prison?" New York: Russell Sage Foundation.

Raphael, Steven and Rudolph Winter-Ebmer. 2001. "Identifying the Effect of Unemployment on Crime." *Journal of Law and Economics* 44(1): 259-283.

Rehavi, M. Marit, and Sonja B. Starr. 2014. "Racial Disparity in Federal Criminal Sentences." *Journal of Political Economy* 122(6): 1320-1354.

Reyes, Jessica Wolpaw. 2007. "Environmental Policy as Social Policy? The Impact of Childhood Lead Exposure on Crime." Working Paper 13097. *National Bureau of Economic Research*.

Reynolds, Arthur J., Judy A. Temple, Dylan L. Robertson, and Emily A. Mann. 2001. "Long-term Effects of an Early Childhood Intervention on Educational Achievement and Juvenile Arrest." *Journal of the American Medical Association* 285(18): 2339-2346.

Roberts, Brent W., Peter D. Harms, Avshalom Caspi, and Terri E. Moffitt. 2007. "Predicting the Counterproductive Employee in a Child-to-Adult Prospective Study." *Journal of Applied Psychology* 92(5): 1427-1436.

Rodriguez, Nino and Brenner Brown. 2003. "Preventing Homelessness Among People Leaving Prison." Vera Institute of Justice.

Rodriguez, Michelle Natividad and Maurice Emsellem. 2011. "65 Million 'Need Not Apply:' The Case for Reforming Criminal Background Checks for Employment." *The National Employment Law Project*.

Roeder, Oliver, Lauren-Brooke Eisen, and Julia Bowling. 2015. "What Caused the Crime Decline?" *Brennan Center for Justice*.

Sabol, William J. 2007. "Local labor market conditions and post-prison employment: Evidence from Ohio." Bureau of Justice Statistics. Working Paper.

Sampson, Robert J., and John H. Laub. 2004. "Life-Course Desisters? Trajectories of Crime Among Delinquent Boys Followed to Age 70." *Criminology* 41(3): 301-340.

Schweinhart, Lawrence J., Jeanne Montie, Zongping Xiang, W. Steven Barnett, Clive R. Belfield, Milagros Nores. 2005. "The High/Scope Perry Preschool Study Through Age 40: Summary Conclusions, and Frequently Asked Questions." Based on *Lifetime Effects: The High/Scope Perry Preschool Study Through Age 40,* Lawrence J. Schweinhart, Jeanne Montie, Zongping Xiang, W. Steven Barnett, Clive R. Belfield, and Milagros Nores, 194-215. Ypsilanti, MI: High/Scope Press.

Seroczynski, A.D., William N. Evans, Amy D. Jobst, Luke Horvath, and Giuliana Carozza. 2015. "Reading for Life and Adolescent Re-Arrest: Evaluating a Unique Juvenile Diversion Program." Working Paper.

Shi, Lan. 2009. "The limit of oversight in policing: Evidence from the 2001 Cincinnati Riot." *Journal of Public Economics* 93(1-2): 99-113.

Society for Human Resource Management. 2012. "The Use of Criminal Background Checks in Hiring Decisions." *The Society for Human Resource Management.*

Spelman, William. 2000. "What Recent Studies Do (and Don't) Tell Us about Imprisonment and Crime." *Justice and Crime* 27(2000). 419-494.

Spelman, William. 2005. "Jobs or Jails? The Crime Drop in Texas." *Journal of Policy Analysis and Management* 27(1). 133-165.

Subramanian, Ram, Ruth Delaney, Stephen Roberts, Nancy Fishman, and Peggy McGarry. February 2015. "Incarceration's Front Door: The Misuse of Jails in America." *VERA Institute of Justice.*

Tittle, Charles R., David A. Ward, and Harold G. Grasmick. 2003. "Gender, Age, and Crime/Deviance: A Challenge to Self-Control Theory." *Journal of Research in Crime and Delinquency* 40(4): 426-453.

Travis, Jeremy, Bruce Western, and Steve Redburn. *The Growth of Incarceration in the United States.* Washington, D.C.: The National Academies Press, 2014.

Truman, Jennifer and Lynn Langton. 2015. "Criminal Victimization, 2014." *Bureau of Justice Statistics, U.S. Department of Justice.*

Tyler, John. H and Jeffrey R. Kling. 2007. "Prison-Based Education and Reentry into the Mainstream Labor Market." *Barriers to reentry?: the labor market for released prisoners in post-industrial America. Edited by Shawn Bushway*, Michael A. Stoll, David Weiman. New York: The Russell Sage Foundation.

U.S. Department of Justice. 2015. "U.S. Department of Justice Report and Recommendations Concerning the Use of Restrictive Housing."

U.S. Government Accountability Office. 2005. "Adult drug courts: Evidence indicates recidivism reductions and mixed results for other outcomes" No. GAO-05-219. Washington, DC.

United States Sentencing Commission (USSC). 2014. "Sensible Sentencing Reform: The 2014 reduction of Drug Sentences." *United States Sentencing Commission.* <http://www.ussc.gov/sites/default/files/pdf/research-and-publications/backgrounders/profile_2014_drug_amendment.pdf>.

United States Sentencing Commission (USSC). 2016. "Recidivism Among Federal Offenders: A Comprehensive Overview." *United States Sentencing Commission.*

U.S. Census. 2015. "State and County QuickFacts." *U.S Census Bureau.* <http://quickfacts.census.gov/qfd/states/00000.html>.

U.S. Department of Housing and Urban Development. 2015. "Guidance for Public Housing Agencies (PHAs) and Owners of Federally-Assisted Housing on Excluding the Use of Arrest Records in Housing Decisions." Office of Public and Indian Housing.

Vallas, Rebecca and Sharon Dietrich. 2014. "One Strike and You're Out: How We Can Eliminate Barriers to Economic Security and Mobility for People with Criminal Records." *Center for American Progress.*

Viscusi, W. Kip. 2000. "The Value of Life in Legal Contexts: Survey and Critique." *American Law and Economics Review* 2(1): 195-222.

Walmsley, Roy. 2016. "World Prison Population List (11th Edition)." *Institute for Criminal Policy Research*.

Webster, Cheryl Marie, Anthony N. Doob, and Franklin E. Zimring. 2006. "Proposition 8 and Crime Rates in California: The Case of the Disappearing Deterrent." *Criminology & Public Policy* 5(3): 417-442.

Weiner, David A., Byron F. Lutz, and Jens Ludwig. 2009. "The Effects of School Desegregation on Crime." Working Paper 15380, *National Bureau of Economic Research*.

Weisburd, David, Cody W. Telep, Joshua C. Hinkle, and John E. Elk. 2010. "Is problem-oriented policing effective in reducing crime and disorder?" *Criminology & Public Policy* 9(1):139-172.

Weiss, Joanna Cohn. 2006. "Tough on Crime: How Campaigns for State Judiciary Violate Criminal Defendants' Due Process Rights." *New York University Law Review* 81(1): 1101-1136.

Western, Bruce. 2002. "The Impact of Incarceration on Wage Mobility and Inequality." *American Sociological Review* 67(4): 526-546.

Western, Bruce and Becky Pettit. 2005. "Black-White Wage Inequality, Employment Rates, and Incarceration." *American Journal of Sociology* 111 (2): 553-578.

Western, Bruce, Anthony A. Braga, Jaclyn Davis, and Catherine Sirois. 2014. "Stress and Hardship After Prison."

Wildeman, Christopher. 2010. "Paternal Incarceration and Children's Physically Aggressive Behaviors: Evidence from the Fragile Families and Child Wellbeing Study." *Social Forces* 89(1): 285-309.

Wilper, Andrew P., Steffie Woolhandler, J. Wesley Boyd, Karen E. Lasser, Danny McCormick, David H. Bor, and David U. Himmelstein. 2009. "The Health and Health Care of US Prisoners: Results of a Nationwide Survey." *American Journal of Public Health* 99 (4): 666-672.